KIDS

WITHDRAWN

LOVE

Kentucky

4TH Edition

Your Family Travel Guide to Exploring
"Kid-Friendly" Kentucky

400 Fun Stops & Unique Spots

Dedicated to the Families of Kentucky

© Copyright 2016, Kids Love Publications, LLC

For the latest major updates corresponding to the pages in this book visit our website: www.KidsLoveTravel.com

- ❑ *REMEMBER: Museum exhibits change frequently. Check the site's website before you visit to note any changes. Also, HOURS and ADMISSIONS are subject to change at the owner's discretion. If you are tight on time or money, check the attraction's website or call before you visit.*

- ❑ *INTERNET PRECAUTION: All websites mentioned in KIDS LOVE KENTUCKY have been checked for appropriate content. However, due to the fast-changing nature of the Internet, we strongly urge parents to preview any recommended sites and to always supervise their children when on-line.*

- ❑ *EDUCATORS: There are suggestions for finding FREE lessons plans embedded in many listings as helpful notes for educators.*

ISBN-13: 978-0692606049

TABLE OF CONTENTS

State Map

(With Major Routes and Cities Marked)

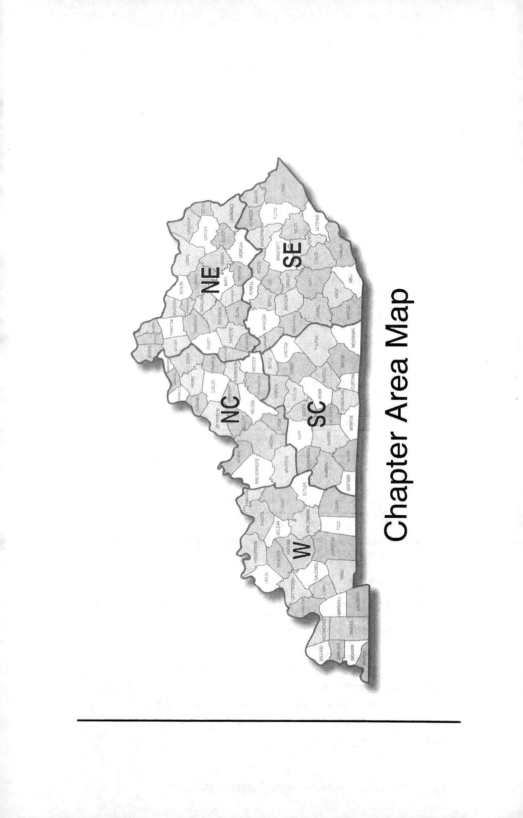

Chapter Area Map

HOW TO USE THIS BOOK

(A few hints to make your adventures run smoothly:)

BEFORE YOU LEAVE:

Each chapter represents a two hour radius area of the state or a Day Trip. The chapter begins with an introduction and Quick Tour of favorites within the chapter. The listings are by City and then alphabetical by name, numeric by zip code. Each listing has tons of important details (pricing, hours, website, etc.) and a review noting the most engaging aspects of the place. Our popular Activity Index in back is helpful if you want to focus on a particular type of attraction (i.e. History, Tours, Outdoor Exploring, Animals & Farms, etc.).

Begin by assigning each family member a different colored highlighter (for example: Daniel gets blue, Jenny gets pink, Mommy gets yellow and Daddy gets green). At your leisure, begin to read each review and put a highlighter "check" mark next to the sites that most interest each family member or highlight the features you most want to see. Now, when you go to plan a quick trip - or a long van ride - you can easily choose different stops in one day to please everyone.

Know directions and parking. Use a GPS system or print off directions from websites.

Most attractions are closed major holidays unless noted.

When children are in tow, it is better to make your lodging reservations ahead of time. Every time we've tried to "wing it", we've always ended up at a place that was overpriced, in an unsafe area, or not super clean. We've never been satisfied when we didn't make a reservation ahead of time.

If you have a large family, or are traveling with extended family or friends, most places offer group discounts. Check out the company's website for details.

For the latest critical updates corresponding to the pages in this book, visit our website: **www.kidslovetravel.com** Click on *Updates*.

ON THE ROAD:

Consider the child's age before you stop at an exit. Some attractions and restaurants, even hotels, are too formal for young ones or not enough of an adventure for teens. Read our trusted reviews first.

Estimate the duration of the trip and how many stops you can afford to make. From our experience, it is best to stop every two hours to stretch your legs or eat/snack or maybe visit an inexpensive attraction.

Bring along travel books and games for "quiet time" in the van. (See tested travel products on **www.kidslovetravel.com**) As an added bonus, these "enriching" games also stimulate conversation - you may get to know your family better and create memorable life lessons

In between meals, we offer the family snacks like: pretzels, whole grain
    chips, nuts, water bottles, bite-size (dark) chocolates, grapes and
    apples. None of these are messy and all are healthy.
Plan picnics along the way. Many Historical sites and State Parks are
    scattered along the highway. Allow time for a rest stop or a scenic
    byway to take advantage of these free picnic facilities.

WAYS TO SAVE MONEY:

Memberships - many children's museums, science centers, zoos and
    aquariums are members of associations that provide FREE or
    Discounted reciprocity to other such museums across the country. AAA
    Auto Club cards offer discounts to many of the activities and hotels in
    this book. If grandparents are along for the ride, they can use their
    AARP card and get discounts. Be sure to carry your member cards with
    you as proof to receive the discounts.
Supermarket Customer Cards - national and local supermarkets often offer
    good discounted tickets to major attractions in the area.
Internet Hotel Reservations - if you're traveling with kids, don't take the risk
    of being spontaneous with lodging. Make reservations ahead of time.
    We don't use non-refundable, deep discount hotel "scouting" websites
    (ex. Hotwire). You can't cancel your reservation, or change them, and
    you can't be guaranteed the type of room you want (ex. non-smoking,
    two beds). Instead, stick with a national hotel chain you trust and join
    their rewards program.
State Travel Centers - as you enter a new state, their welcome centers offer
    many current promotions.
Hotel Lobbies - often have a display of discount coupons to area shops and
    restaurants. When you check in, ask the clerk for discount pizza
    coupons they may have at the front desk.
Attraction Online Coupons - check the websites listed with each review for
possible printable coupons or discounted online tickets good towards the
attraction.

GENERAL INFORMATION

Call *(or visit the websites)* for the services of interest. Request email updates.

- ❑ Canoe Kentucky (800) K-CANOE -1 or **www.canoeky.com**
- ❑ Kentucky Arts Council, **www.kyarts.org**
- ❑ Kentucky Roadside Farm Markets **www.kyfb.com/roadside.htm**
- ❑ Kentucky State Parks (800) 255-Park or **www.parks.ky.gov**
- ❑ Kentucky Tourism Council, **www.kentuckytourism.com** or (800)
     225-8747
- ❑ Louisville CVB **www.gotolouisville.com**
- ❑ Lexington CVB **www.visitlex.com**
- ❑ KY Dept of Fish & Wildlife: (502) 564-4336 or
     www.kdfwr.state.ky.us

STATE NATURE PRESERVES
- ❑ Phone: (502) 573-2886 **wwwkynaturepreserves.org**
- ❑ Hours: Dawn to dusk, daily. Admission: FREE. Open to the public for hiking, birding and nature study.

NC - <u>VERNON-DOUGLAS STATE NATURE PRESERVE</u> - Elizabethtown, off KY 583. Mature second growth forest with rich array of spring wildflowers.

NC - <u>BEARGRASS CREEK STATE NATURE PRESERVE</u> at the Louisville Nature Center - Louisville, 1297 Trevilian Way. (502) 458-1328. Over 40 acres of mature forest, adjacent to Creason Park, popular for birding in an urban setting.

NE - <u>BOONE COUNTY CLIFFS STATE NATURE PRESERVE</u> - Burlington, I-75 to KY 18 west. 20-40' cliffs formed from the gravel washed out of melting glaciers north of the area can be seen.

NE - <u>DINSMORE WOODS STATE NATURE PRESERVE</u> - Burlington, I-75 exit 181 to KY 18 west. Park at Middle Creek Park. Fairly undisturbed old growth mixed hardwood forest which hosts various spring wildflowers.

NE - <u>QUIET TRAILS STATE NATURE PRESERVE</u> - Cynthiana, off Pugh's Ferry Road, near Sunrise, on the Licking river. Birds, trees & wildflowers, over 20 species of mussels come from the river.

NE - <u>JESSE STUART STATE NATURE PRESERVE</u> - Greenup, West Hollow Road, off KY 1. Known as W-Hollow, it was home to the internationally known author, Jesse Stuart.

NE - <u>TOM DORMAN STATE NATURE PRESERVE</u> - Nicholasville, US 27S to KY 1845. Forested slopes of spring wildflowers on spectacular 300' cliffs across the Kentucky River.

SE - <u>PILOT KNOB STATE NATURE PRESERVE</u> - Clay City, Mountain Pkwy, exit 16. One of the tallest knobs in the Cumberland Plateau. It's considered to be the place where Daniel Boone first stood and looked over the Bluegrass. Hiking here, too.

SE - <u>BAD BRANCH STATE NATURE PRESERVE</u> - Whitesburg, KY 932. Over 1000 acres of forested gorge containing a 60 foot waterfall, rare plants and animals.

W - <u>METROPOLIS LAKE STATE NATURE PRESERVE</u> - Paducah, off KY 996. Find five species of rare fish, beaver wintering place for bald eagles in a lake ringed with balk cypress and swamp tupelo.

W - <u>LOGAN COUNTY - GLADE STATE NATURE PRESERVE</u> - Russellville, off US 68/KY 80. Over 40 acres with limestone glades and a 810 foot knob. The rocky slopes are adorned with prairie grasses and rare plants like Carolina Larkspur, Glade violet.

NE - <u>ANDERSON FERRY</u> - Florence, KY8. Crosses Ohio River to US 50 in Ohio. Hours 6:00am-8:00pm (November-April) and 6:00am-9:30pm (May-October). Open 7:00am on Sundays & holidays. Fare: $3.00 per car.

NE - <u>VALLEY VIEW FERRY</u> - Nicholasville, KY 169E at the Kentucky River. The oldest continuous business in Kentucky since 1785. FREE.

SC - <u>CUMBERLAND RIVER FERRY</u> - Tompkinsville, KY 214. Kentucky's only state-operated ferry running 24 hours a day to scenic Turkey Neck Bend.

W - <u>HICKMAN-DORENA FERRY</u> - Hickman, Off KY 94. Ferry crosses the Mississippi river from Hickman to Dorena, MO. Runs daily except Christmas. 7:00am-6:15pm (April-October), 7:00am-5:00pm (November-March). Fare $8.00 per car.

W - <u>CAVE IN ROCK FERRY</u> - Marion, KY 91. Crosses Ohio River to Illinois. FREE

Check out these businesses / services for tour ideas:

<u>ANIMAL SHELTERS</u> - Great for the would-be pet owner. Not only will you see many cats and dogs available for adoption, but a guide will show you the clinic and explain the needs of a pet. Be prepared to have the children "fall in love" with one of the animals while they are there!

<u>BANKS</u> - Take a "behind the scenes" look at automated teller machines, bank vaults and drive-thru window chutes. You may want to take this tour and then open a savings account for your child.

<u>CITY HALLS</u> - Halls of Fame, City Council Chambers & Meeting Room, Mayor's Office and famous statues.

<u>FIRE STATIONS</u> - Open Houses in October, Fire Prevention Month. Take a look into the life of the firefighters servicing your area and try on their gear. See where they hang out, sleep and eat. Hop aboard a real-life fire engine truck and learn fire safety too.

<u>HOSPITALS</u> - Children's Hospitals offer pre-surgery and general tours.

<u>NEWSPAPERS</u> - See monster printers and robotics. See samples in the layout department and maybe try to put together your own page. After seeing a newspaper made, most companies give you a free copy (dated that day) as your souvenir. National Newspaper Week is in October.

<u>PETCO</u> - Contact each store manager to see if they participate. The Fur, Feathers & Fins™ program allows children to learn about the characteristics and habitats of fish, reptiles, birds, and small animals. At your local Petco, lessons in science, math and geography come to life through this hands-on field trip.

KIDS LOVE KENTUCKY

PIZZA HUT & PAPA JOHN'S - Participating locations. Telephone the store manager. Best days are Monday, Tuesday and Wednesday mid-afternoon. Minimum of 10 people. Small charge per person. All children love pizza – especially when they can create their own! As the children tour the kitchen, they learn how to make a pizza, bake it, and then eat it. The admission charge generally includes lots of creatively made pizzas, beverage and coloring book.

KRISPY KREME DONUTS - Participating locations. Get an "inside look" and learn the techniques that make these donuts some of our favorites! Watch the dough being made in "giant" mixers, being formed into donuts and taking a "trip" through the fryer. Seeing them being iced and topped with colorful sprinkles is always a favorite with the kids. Contact your local store manager. They prefer Monday or Tuesday. Free.

SUPERMARKETS - Kids are fascinated to go behind the scenes of the same store where Mom and Dad shop. Usually you will see them grind meat, walk into large freezer rooms, watch cakes and bread bake and receive free samples along the way. Maybe you'll even get to pet a live lobster!

TV / RADIO STATIONS - Studios, newsrooms, Fox kids clubs. Why do weathermen never wear blue/green clothes on TV? What makes a "DJ's" voice sound so deep and smooth?

WATER TREATMENT PLANTS - A giant science experiment! You can watch seven stages of water treatment. The favorite is usually the wall of bright buttons flashing as workers monitor the different processes.

U.S. MAIN POST OFFICES - Did you know Ben Franklin was the first Postmaster General (over 200 years ago)? Most interesting is the high-speed automated mail processing equipment. Learn how to address envelopes so they will be sent quicker (there are secrets). To make your tour more interesting, have your children write a letter to themselves and address it with colorful markers. Mail it earlier that day and they will stay interested trying to locate their letter in all the high-speed machinery.

1

Chapter 1
Area - North Central (NC)

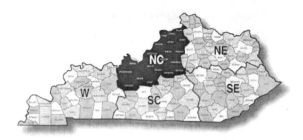

2

Our Favorites...

* My Old Kentucky Home - Bardstown
* Kentucky History Center - Frankfort
* Rebecca Ruth Candy - Frankfort
* Salato Wildlife Education Center - Frankfort
* "Daniel Boone - The Man & The Legend" and
Old Fort Harrod - Harrodsburg
* Lincoln Birthplace & Museum - Hodgenville
* American Printing House for the Blind - Louisville
* Louisville Slugger Museum - Louisville
* Pottery Tours - Louisville
* Kentucky Railway Museum - New Haven

Pioneer Cookin'
with Daniel & Jenny
- Old Fort Harrod

A QUICK TOUR OF FRANKFORT & LOUISVILLE

If you haven't already, every Kentucky family should visit the hub of history in Frankfort. Begin with natural history at Salato Wildlife Education Center on US 60. Interactive and interpretive exhibits feature native Kentucky plants and animals. View KY Record Fish mounted on storyboards. Just around the corner is the most unique site – have you ever seen a live Alligator Snapping Turtle? Outdoors, walk trails past American Bald Eagles, white-tailed deer, wild turkeys, bison, elk and bobcat.

At the History Center, take "A Kentucky Journey". Explore ten distinct time periods in history – touching all regions, counties and people of the state. Begin in the Cumberland Gap, next, on to the woodlands to the pioneers to walk-thru flat boats. Research the Battle of Perrysville or the "houses divided" in the Civil War or unusual inventions or maybe explore a simulated coal mine. Do you know which famous people and companies started in Kentucky?

Starting on the Ohio River, begin a day trip at the Louisville Science Center or Louisville Slugger Museum. Both museums have many hands-on areas. Families can: Be-in-a-Bubble, "Hop On" a bus, "Take Off" in a plane (the Science Museum's KIDZONE is outstanding), climb on a giant ball and glove, "Play Ball", experience a 90 mph pitch, or, watch wood cylinders magically swirled into branded bats.

After lunch at Camberly Brown Hotel for the famous "Hot Browns" sandwiches, purchase a ticket to the Belle of Louisville Sightseeing Cruise. This national landmark is powered by two steam engines and has open-air and enclosed decks. As the steam calliope pipes its farewell whistle, you'll begin a river tour narrated by a "ghost" captain. He or she will talk of olden days and point out special interesting sites like the Falls of the Ohio fossil bed or famous bridges and shipyards.

Day two in Louisville might take you to historic places. Louisville Stoneware Company and Hadley Pottery are both east of town and both offer tours of their famous hand-painted pottery factories. Whimsical designs and clay stacked high to the ceiling are the kid's favorite areas. After you've watched artists create beautiful works, create you own.

Another very interesting factory tour, east of downtown, is the American Printing House for the Blind. You'll start in the hands-on area where visitors can actually learn some of the Braille alphabet, read a popular book in both Braille and written word, or test a talking color analyzer that helps the color-blind match their clothing. Next, briefly tour the plant where they print, bind and proofread. Finish in the museum. They have on display their largest Braille project ever – The World Book Encyclopedia.

Not too far from the Printing House & Hadley Pottery is Thomas Edison's House. The guides here will highlight many points of the famous inventor's life – especially before he became famous.

NC CHAPTER AT A GLANCE...

BARDSTOWN
Civil War Museum
My Old Kentucky Home
Stephen Foster, the Musical
Old Talbott Tavern
CARROLLTON
General Butler St Resort Park
ELIZABETHTOWN
Freeman Lake Park
Historic Downtown Walking Tour
Swopes Cars
FALLS OF ROUGH
Rough River Dam St Resort Park
FORT KNOX
Gold Vault
Patton Museum of Cavalry & Armor
FRANKFORT
Frankfort Fish Hatchery
Buckley Wildlife Sanctuary
Country Place Jamboree
Governors Mansion
Kentucky History Center
Kentucky Military History
Kentucky State Capitol
Kentucky State University
Kentucky Vietnam Vet
Leslie Morris Park
Old State Capitol
Rebecca-Ruth Candy
Salato
Vest Lindsey House
Kentucky Book Fair
Kentucky Folklife Festival
Happy Jacks Farm
GOSHEN
Creasey Mahan Nature Preserve
HARRODSBURG
Shaker Village
Dixie Belle Riverboat
Old Fort Harrod St Pk

HODGENVILLE
Abraham Lincoln BP
Lincoln's Birthday
Lincoln Jamboree
Lincoln's Boyhood Home
Lincoln Days
LAWRENCEBURG
Burgoo Festival
LOUISVILLE
Belle of Louisville
Frazier History Museum
Louisville Ballet
Louisville Science Ctr
Louisville Slugger Mus
Stage One
Thomas Edison House
Louisville Stoneware
American Printing House for Blind
Hadley Pottery
Locust Grove
Kentucky Derby Museum
Speed Art Museum
Hilton Garden Inn Louisville
Portland Museum
Louisville Zoo
MegaCaverns
Music Theatre Louisville
Hawks View Glass
Louisville River Bats
EP Tom Sawyer St Pk
Kentucky Derby Festival
Waterfront Independence Festival
Kentucky State Fair
Festival of Trees & Lights
Bernheim Forest
Jefferson Memorial Forest
Henrys Ark
Springhill Suites
NEW HAVEN
Kentucky Railway Museum
SPARTA
Kentucky Speedway
SPRINGFIELD
Lincoln Homestead St Pk
Ky Crossroads Harvest Festival
TAYLORSVILLE
Taylorsville Lake St Pk

CIVIL WAR MUSEUM OF THE WESTERN THEATRE

310 East Broadway (Rte. 60 exit 25 or I-65S exit 112)

Bardstown 40004

- ❏ Phone: (502) 349-0291. **www.civil-war-museum.org/**
- ❏ Hours: Daily 10am – 5pm (March-October). November, weekends only. Closed Easter and Thanksgiving.
- ❏ Admission: $10.00 adult, $5.00 child (6-15) for all four venues.

See artifacts and photographs from Civil War battles fought in Georgia, Kentucky, Tennessee, Mississippi and Missouri. Also see rare flags, uniforms, maps, both North and South weapons and medical equipment. Trace the progression of the war, chronologically (easy to follow). They also have a campsite featuring a wagon actually used during a conflict on a battlefield. Here are some questions to answer when you tour: Why did West Virginia form as a separate state because of the Civil War? The book "Uncle Tom's Cabin" came out before the war started - did the author start the war? Injured in the war? (be careful, they loved to amputate)! Would you want to be a drummer boy? Before you leave, be sure to ask the story about the US belt buckle turned upside down. This museum was voted the 4th best Civil War museum in the nation.

The WOMEN IN CIVIL WAR MUSEUM is just up the street. Learn why early nurses were only nuns or plain spinsters; learn why women were the ones to realize more sanitary conditions were needed (famous Clara Barton, Elizabeth Blackwell); and especially learn why women were the best spies!

HISTORIC BARDSTOWN VILLAGE is next door with authentic cabins to peek in. Self-guided tours.

MUSEUM OF MIDAMERICA features exhibits covering conflicts from the American Revolution to the mid-East battles of today, centered around contributions of Kentuckians.

LIVING HISTORY AND CIVIL WAR SHOW

Drills portraying the Battle of Bardstown in the Civil War. Soldiers in uniform and ladies in period costume. (Saturday in mid-July)

MY OLD KENTUCKY HOME STATE PARK

US 150 Springfield Road (off the Bluegrass Pkwy, just east of downtown)

Bardstown 40004

❑ Phone: (502) 348-3502

http://parks.ky.gov/parks/recreationparks/old-ky-home/default.aspx

❑ Admission: Kentucky State Parks do not charge admission to grounds.

❑ Tours: $10 adult, $7 child (6-12). Small discount for senior/teens. Daily 9:00am-5:00pm (March-November). Wednesday-Sunday only in January & February. Closed Thanksgiving, week of Christmas and New Years.

❑ Note: Gift shop, picnic, playground and camping. Tours every fifteen minutes.

The stately Georgian Colonial mansion is most famous because it is the inspiration for Stephen Foster's famous ballad "My Old Kentucky Home" - the official Kentucky state song. It was the home of Judge John Rowan whose Pittsburgh cousin, Stephen Foster, visited in 1852. Visit the days of the antebellum South as costumed guides escort you through the restored mansion, formal gardens, carriage house and smokehouse. Here are some unique things for the kids to look for while on tour: 13 foot high and 13 inch thick walls, 13 windows and 13 steps because of the 13 original colonies; see the "napping couch and Day Bed"; look for the "hip bath" for bathing in the kids' rooms; learn why children ate upstairs in the hallway; or look for the picture that follows you.

CHRISTMAS CANDLELIGHT TOURS

Sample the elegant past during "My Old Kentucky Home" annual Christmas Candlelight tours. The glow of candlelight will adorn the mansion in splendid 1800's fashion. Elaborate period holiday costumes, music and traditional refreshments nightly. The Park's Gift Shop offers unique Kentucky handmade crafts, foods and holiday gifts. Admission. (weekends in December)

STEPHEN FOSTER - THE MUSICAL

US 150 east of downtown (Bluegrass Pkwy. On grounds of "My Old Kentucky Home")

Bardstown 40004

❑　Phone: (502) 348-5971 or (800) 626-1563
www.stephenfoster.com

❑　Hours: Tuesday-Sunday 8:00pm nightly (outdoor theatre, indoors if inclement weather). Saturday matinees at 2:00pm, indoors. (early June-late August). Wednesday, Thursday and Sunday evening shows are usually another famous musical vs. Stephen Foster. Check website for details of specific dates. EDT

❑　Admission: $18.00-$25.00 adult, ~ Half price for child (6-12). FREE for children 6 and under. Online coupons.

❑　Note: The shows last over 2 hours. You may want to consider your child's attention span - especially late evening.

Performed under the stars for a romantic setting, this is a good follow up to your tour of My Old Kentucky Home up on the hill above the theatre. Spectacular period costumes, lively music, dances and more than 50 toe-stomping Foster songs including "Camptown Races" and "Oh, Susanna" - everyone knows them. Did you know Foster was America's first great composer?

OLD TALBOTT TAVERN

107 West Stephen Foster Avenue (Court Square)

Bardstown 40004

❑　Phone: (800) 4-Tavern **http://www.talbotts.com/**
❑　Hours: Lunch and Dinner daily.
❑　Admission: Moderate to high priced menu.
❑　Note: Bed & Breakfast and Gift Shop. Just browse if you like. Another place you can get a Kentucky Hot Brown.

Mid-America's oldest stagecoach stop where historic recipe meals are still served today. It's the oldest inn (1779) in continuous operation located west of the Alleghenies. Notables such as Louis Phillippe, John Audubon, and George Rogers Clark rested here on their journeys and you can see bullet holes shot by Jesse James! Choose from Fried Green Tomatoes, Burgoo, Mrs. Eleanor's Fried Chicken or Country Ham.

After you order (or while you're waiting to be seated), take a self-guided look around. Although it's historic, it's unusually very kid-friendly. Wait staff are dressed in period and there's a great, fun children's menu.

GENERAL BUTLER STATE RESORT PARK

PO Box 325 (I-71 at Carrollton - KY 227, 44 miles northeast of Louisville)

Carrollton 41008

❑ Phone: (502) 732-4384 or (866) GO-Butler (reservations)
http://parks.ky.gov/parks/resortparks/general-butler/default.aspx
❑ Admission: FREE. Fee for tours.
❑ Note: Play it Again in the Park evening concerts (select summer Saturdays).

This resort pays tribute to one of Kentucky's foremost military families, namely General William Orlando Butler. Beginning in colonial times through the Civil War, the military fame of the Butler family is known well and displayed at the Butler-Turpin Historic House. See the 1859 furnished home full of heirlooms. Along with the historic house and summer kitchen built in 1859, is the archaeology of the log house, the Butler Family Cemetery and the surrounding grounds that was once the Butler farm. (Tours are February-December, three times daily for $3-$5.00 admission).

Also in the park is a hilltop lodge (53 rooms), short nature trails, tennis, cottages, a campground, a marina, rental boats, a pool and beach, mini-golf and recreation programs. The Lodge is open daily except Winter Hours start Wednesday evening thru Sunday afternoon. Two Rivers' Restaurant name and fish camp décor is a reference to the Ohio and Kentucky rivers which meet in the local area. Two Rivers restaurant serves a bistro style dinner menu with a variety of items ranging from fish to pasta and chicken to steaks. They also serve our signature Kentucky favorites and locally grown produce.

KENTUCKY SCOTTISH WEEKEND

General Butler SRP. **http://www.kyscottishweekend.org/**. The state celebrates many with Scottish heritage with athletic competitions, games, contests (how about the boniest knees contest?). Highland dancing and food. Saturday night Ceilidl and Sunday Kirkin' of the Tartan. Admission. (Mothers Day weekend in May)

FESTIVAL OF TREES & WINTER WONDERFEST DAY

General Butler SRP. Christmas Trees decorated by local schools, churches, organizations and businesses will adorn the Butler Lodge, to help ring-in the holiday season. Winter Wonderfest Day is full of surprises for the young and young at heart! Santa will be featured for Breakfast on Saturday morning; along with morning activities in the Lodge Lounge and an evening holiday concert. FREE. (first weekend in December)

FREEMAN LAKE PARK

North US 31 W

Elizabethtown 42701

❑   Phone: (270) 769-3916 or

      http://www.elizabethtownky.org/freeman-lake-park.asp
❑   Hours: Park open 8:00am-dusk. Homes open Saturday 10:00am-
      6:00pm, Sunday 1:00-6:00pm (June-September).
❑   Admission: Donations

On the campus of this park are three historic homes. The Lincoln Heritage House is a double log house crafted in part by Abraham Lincoln's father. The Sarah Bush Johnston Lincoln Memorial Cabin is a replica of the home of Sarah Bush Johnston's Elizabethtown home at the time she married Thomas Lincoln. Finally, the One Room School House was originally built in Summitt, KY in 1892 and considered the finest school in the county. The park also has fishing, playgrounds, picnic areas, canoe, rowboat, and pedal boat rental.

FESTIVAL OF LIGHTS

Freeman Lake Park. (Thanksgiving - December evenings)

HISTORIC DOWNTOWN ELIZABETHTOWN WALKING TOUR

Downtown, **Elizabethtown** 42701

❑   Phone: (270) 982-2209 or **www.touretown.com**
❑   Hours: Thursday at 7:00pm (June-September)
❑   Admission: FREE

The tour walks along 25 historic sites and buildings. Along the way, historical characters dramatically reveal their part in the town's history (with characters like General Custer). It's a whimsical "meet and greet" and a great way for kids to understand the personalities behind the history.

SWOPE'S CARS OF YESTERYEAR MUSEUM

1100 North Dixie Avenue (US 31W)

Elizabethtown 42701

❑   Phone: (270) 765-2181. **www.swopemuseum.com**
❑   Hours: Monday-Saturday 10:00am-5:00pm. Closed Sundays and holidays.
❑   Admission: FREE

Wonderful machines of yesteryear (approx. 50) are on display. Most of the cars are from the 20s, 30s and 40s, and even a few from the 50s and 60s. Good nostalgia walk with grandparents at the lead. Take the time to listen to their memories…

ROUGH RIVER DAM STATE RESORT PARK

450 Lodge Road (Western Parkway to KY 79 north at Caneyville)

Falls of Rough 40119

❑   Phone: (270) 257-2311 or (800) 325-1713
        http://parks.ky.gov/parks/resortparks/rough-river/default.aspx
❑   Hours: Lodge open daily spring thru fall. Open Wednesday-Sunday only (winters).
❑   Note: Pine Knob Theatre - musical comedy and folklore, Friday & Saturday nights, June-September. Phone: (270) 879-8190. All seats $10.00-$15.00. Reservations are not required unless groups. **Www.pineknob.com**.

Fine fishing waters can be found in the deep waters of Rough River. Fishing or not, there's also boat rentals, a lodge, cottages, dining (famous for catfish), a beach, campgrounds, some hiking trails, tennis, golf, mini-golf and recreation programs surrounding the approximately 5000 acre lake. Enjoy the history of the area at old Falls of Rough, a quaint 19th century mill community along the self-guided interpretive trail (Folklore Trail-0.7 mile loop).

GOLD VAULT - US BULLION DEPOSITORY

(View the Vault from US 31W and Bullion Blvd. On Fort Knox)

Fort Knox 40121

❑   Phone: (800) 334-7540

Constructed in 1936 at a cost of $560,000, the 2 level vault with door (weighing 20 tons) is guarded 24 hours a day. Made of granite, steel and concrete, its dimensions are 105 by 121 feet. Gold in the depository is in the form of standard mint bars somewhat smaller than a building brick - each brick weighs about 27.5 pounds. The Mint is guarded 24 hours a day. No visitors are allowed (unless you are a United States President or high level cabinet member)…but pictures may be taken of the outside of the building.

PATTON MUSEUM OF CAVALRY & ARMOR

4554 Fayette Avenue

Fort Knox 40121

❑   Phone: (502) 624-3812. **www.generalpatton.org**
❑   Hours: Tuesday-Friday 9:00am-4:30pm. Saturday and Federal
       Holidays 10:00am-5:30pm. Closed Christmastime and New Years
       time, Easter, Thanksgiving.
❑   Admission: FREE
❑   FREEBIES: here's a page of interactive quizzes about army life, war
       and leadership: **www.generalpatton.org/education/interactive.asp** .
       Educators: lesson plans -
       www.generalpatton.org/education/programs.asp

A museum of military history of armor and cavalry. You'll see General George S. Patton's personal belongings, a modified Patton jeep, Patton's office van, and a Sherman tank. Learn about the history of the

Gold Vault. The highlight for kids is probably the American and Foreign armored vehicles and uniforms - how they've changed. Most are displayed outside. The largest tank was never used - why? Military (mini) dioramas (with little army men) depict offensive and defensive strategies.

BUCKLEY WILDLIFE SANCTUARY

1035 Germany Road
(I-64 exit 58, US 60 east, KY 1681, 1650 & 1964),

Frankfort 40601

❑   Phone: (859) 873-5711 **www.buckleyhills.org**
❑   Hours: Wednesday-Friday 9:00am-5:00pm, Saturday & Sunday
     9:00am-6:00pm. Closed holidays. Nature Center Building & Gift shop
     open weekends only 1:00-6:00pm and for special programs. Closed
     January and February.
❑   Admission: $3.00-$4.00 per person. Prices for special events vary.

Observe wildlife at the bird blind, hiking trails, fields, forests and wet areas. Operated by the National Audubon Society, three trails meander along the Kentucky River and bluegrass...havens for birds, mammals and wildflowers. The dramatic gorge exposes limestone imbedded marine fossils.

FRANKFORT FISH HATCHERY

Indian Gap Road, north off US 127 near Swallowfield

Frankfort 40601

❑   Phone: (502) 564-4957 **www.wildlifeviewingareas.com/wv-**
     app/ParkDetail.aspx?ParkID=244
❑   Hours: Monday-Friday 7:00am-3:00pm for self-guided tours. Group
     tours by appointment.
❑   Admission: FREE
❑   Tours: Guided and self-guided.
❑   Note: April, May and June are best for observing hatchery in full
     operation.

Rearing ponds, hatching house, and a feed office occupy the land where fish are raised to stock farm ponds and public lakes and for research. Although no attempt is made to produce albino catfish, visitors can see specimens in several of the hatcheries 45 rearing ponds. A research project on freshwater mussels may also be viewed. An outside display pool, maintained March to November, contains bass, bluegill, hybrid striped bass, trout, paddlefish, gar, carp, buffalo, crayfish, goldfish, several catfish species, frogs, and a snapping turtle. Wood duck, Canada goose, and wading birds such as great blue and little green heron are common here spring, summer, and fall. Ospreys occasionally visit. The site is excellent for viewing American kestrel, orioles, swallows, and soaring vultures.

Anglers can walk to Elkhorn Creek to fish from the banks (fishing license required). An 11-acre island, owned by the hatchery, splits the waterway.

GOVERNOR'S MANSION

Capital Avenue building Complex (next to the Capitol building and overlooking the KY River)

Frankfort 40601

❑ Phone: (502) 564-3449
www.governorsmansion.ky.gov
❑ Hours: Tuesday & Thursday 9:00-11:00am. Also guided tours available by reservation.
❑ Admission: FREE

Here, sitting in a beautiful setting, is the official Governor's residence. Modeled after Marie Antoinette's summer villa, the rooms you'll see on the tour are the state dining room, ballroom, reception room and formal salon - all rooms designed for "meet and greet" activities.

CENTER FOR KENTUCKY HISTORY

100 West Broadway Street (Downtown)

Frankfort 40601

❑ Phone: (502) 564-1792 **http://history.ky.gov**
❑ Hours: Thursday 10:00am-8:00pm. Tuesday-Saturday 10:00am-5:00pm. Closed state holiday weekends.
❑ Admission: $2.00-$4.00 (age 6+) includes KY Military History Museum and Old State Capital.
❑ Tours: Guided and self-guided.
❑ Note: 1792 Museum Store, a world class genealogical research library,

changing exhibit gallery. Educators: Teachers Guide -
http://history.ky.gov/pdf/Education/Kentucky_Journey_TG_2008. pdf

This large museum includes the most expansive part - the permanent interactive exhibit titled "A Kentucky Journey". Explore 10 distinct time periods in Kentucky history - touching all regions, counties and peoples of the state. Hands-on activities and dioramas include voices and music from that time period. Begin with a lifelike reproduction of the view of the Cumberland Gap. Then, on to: Prehistoric Native Americans hunting in woodlands; Pioneer walk-thru flat boat; Battles of Perryville or the "Houses Divided" in the Civil War; Southern Exposition of 1880 prototypes of very unusual inventions; Simulated Coal Mine; and the Present - George Clooney's scrubs signed by the ER cast, copy of Primetime Live script donated by Diane Sawyer, PapaJohn's Pizza, KFC, Ashland Oil, Corvette and Toyota. There's so much to read and view - all Kentuckians should visit often to learn a little something new each time.

KENTUCKY FOLKLIFE FESTIVAL

www.folklife.ky.gov Celebrate Kentucky folklife with updated demonstrations and exhibits designed to educate and entertain visitors to Kentucky culture, food and musical heritage. Family Folklore tent on the river has many hands-on activities. "A Chance to Dance" teaches visitors new ethnic moves. (last weekend in September)

KENTUCKY MILITARY HISTORY MUSEUM

East Main Street at Capital Avenue (Old State Arsenal, US 60)

Frankfort 40601

❑   Phone: (877) 4-HISTORY **http://history.ky.gov**
❑   Hours: Tuesday-Saturdays 10:00am-5:00pm. Closed winters.
❑   Admission: Included with admission to Center for KY History.

Displays here include a collection of firearms, edged weapons, artillery, and uniforms emphasizing Militia, State Guard, and other organizations from the Revolution through Operation Desert Storm. Mostly geared towards adults or students studying Kentucky's contributions to US Military. Operated by the Kentucky National Guard.

DID YOU KNOW?

Daniel Boone's grave is nearby at 215 East Main Street (Frankfort Cemetery).

KENTUCKY STATE CAPITOL AREA

Capital Avenue

Frankfort 40601

❑ Phone: (502) 564-3449 **http://capitol.ky.gov/Pages/visitorinfo.aspx**

❑ Admission: FREE

❑ Tours: Tuesday-Saturday beginning at 10:30am and then every 1.5 hours. Last tour at 3pm. Winter tours are only on Saturdays. Tours start at the Center for Kentucky History.

❑ Note: Gift shop, Snack Bar (homemade entrée for lunch!)

Completed in 1910, the Beaux Arts design features 70 iconic columns, decorative murals (two of Daniel Boone) and sculptures of Kentucky dignitaries. There is a 212 foot high dome with French influences throughout (Napoleon & Marie Antoinette rooms). Notice all the door knobs bear the state seal. The Floral Clock, located on the West Lawn, is planted with 20,000 colorful flowering plants. The face of this clock is 34 inches in diameter. It's unique because it's tilted above the reflecting pool supported by its 100 ton planter. Throw a coin into the fountain of the clock and make a wish (coins donated to children's charities). Also, the First Lady Doll Collection, changing history and culture exhibits are featured on the first floor. Oh, by the way, be sure to stop by the Governor's Office and peek in. Maybe they'll offer you a "Govern-mint" as a sweet souvenir of you visit.

KENTUCKY STATE UNIVERSITY

East Main Street

Frankfort 40601

❑ Phone: (502) 567-6000. **www.kysu.edu**

❑ Hours: Monday-Friday 8:00am-4:30pm.

❑ Admission: FREE

KSU is a small, liberal studies university founded in 1886. Visit Jackson Hall with its art gallery and Center for Excellence for the Study of Kentucky African Americans. The Blazer Library is open to the public. Most kids will probably gravitate to the Atwood Agricultural Research Facility and its 166 acre research farm and King Farouk butterfly/moth collection. The Environmental Education Center has several habitats to hike, including a pond.

KENTUCKY BOOK FAIR

www.kybookfair.org. Books about Kentucky or authors from Kentucky. Workshops and autographings make for good Christmas gifts. Kentucky State University Exum Center (first or second Saturday in November)

KENTUCKY VIETNAM VETERAN'S MEMORIAL

Coffee Tree Road (Off SRKY 676)

Frankfort 40601

- ❑ Hours: Dawn to dusk
- ❑ Admission: FREE

Overlooking the city, the names of the Kentuckians who died in Vietnam are etched in granite beneath the giant memorial sundial. The point of the sundial's shadow actually touches the veteran's name on the anniversary of his death!… Incredible! Recognized as one of the most original and unusual memorials in the nation, it is truly touching.

LESLIE MORRIS PARK ON FORT HILL

300 Broadway (Old Capitol Annex)

Frankfort 40601

- ❑ Phone: (800) 960-7200
  http://www.capitalcitymuseum.com/html/fort_hill.html
- ❑ Hours: Daylight hours. Visitors Center: Tuesday, Thursday & Saturday 11:00am-4:00pm.
- ❑ Admission: FREE
- ❑ Tours: self guided tours begin at Fort Hill Visitors Center located on the 1st floor of the Annex. Guided tours are offered Tuesday-Saturday (June-October). No restrooms on property.
- ❑ Note: a trail from behind Capital Plaza Tower leads to this park.
- ❑ The trail is actually an unchanged 19th century road

This Civil War site is where local militia held off an attack by Confederate cavalrymen attempting to invade and destroy the capitol of Kentucky. The walls of Fort Boone still stand, as do the earthworks of a second fort known as the New Redoubt. The walking tour points out the 1864 skirmish site. There's a good chance you'll see deer in the forest.

OLD STATE CAPITOL

Broadway and Lewis Street

Frankfort 40601

❑   Phone: (502) 564-1792 **http://history.ky.gov/old-state-capitol/**
❑   Hours: Tuesday-Saturday. Closed Winters and State Holidays.
❑   Admission: $2.00-$4.00 (age 6+).
❑   Tours: Guided tours begin every hour, last tour at 4:00 p.m. Closed
     Sunday and Monday and most major holidays.

This national landmark, operated by the Kentucky Historical Society, was the seat of government from 1830 to 1910. The most interesting part of the structure is the unique, self-supporting staircase held together by pressure of the circular angles. This was the only pro-Union state capitol occupied by the Confederate army during the Civil War and, in 1900, for a time, the place where Kentuckians threatened to fight their own miniature civil war.

REBECCA-RUTH CANDY

112 East Second Street (Downtown & Capital Ave (near Ky River)

Frankfort 40601

❑   Phone: (502) 223-7475 **www.rebeccaruth.com**
❑   Store Hours: Monday-Saturday 8:30am-5:30pm, Sunday Noon-
     5:00pm (Year-round).
❑   Admission: $2.00 per person (age 6+).
❑   Tours: Monday-Saturday 10:00am-Noon or 1:00-5:30pm (Best times
     are before 1:00pm). (April-November). 10 minutes, guided. Walk-ins
     welcome. Tours are not given 4 days prior Valentines, Easter, &
     Mothers Day due to increased business volume.

This candy store business was co-founded in 1919 by two schoolteachers, Rebecca and Ruth. They started in their houses making candy over the holidays. Today Ruth Booe's grandson is owner and hands-on operator of this confectionery (you'll probably bump into him). The highlights include free samples, an educational video, antique cooking furnace with hand-stirred copper kettles, production areas and "Edna's Table". A 12 foot curved marble slab was purchased by Ruth for $10 in 1917, now it's named after Edna, an employee of 67 years (ate candy 'til the day she died). They make 100 varieties of confections including some unique to Kentucky at 1000 pounds/day. Cute, small-town, casual way to spend a few minutes in a candy factory - what fun!

SALATO WILDLIFE EDUCATION CENTER

#1 Game Farm Road (I-64 exit 53B to US 127N to US 60)

Frankfort 40601

- ❑ Phone: (502) 564-7863   **http://fw.ky.gov/Education/Pages/Salato-Wildlife-Education-Center.aspx**
- ❑ Hours: Tuesday-Friday 9:00am-5:00pm, Saturday 10:00am-5:00pm (March-Thanksgiving). Park open sunrise to sunset. Closed most holidays.
- ❑ Admission: $2.00-$4.00 (age 5+)
- ❑ Note: 132 acre complex with public fishing, picnicking and wildlife viewing. Kentucky Afield Gift Shop.

This educational center has interactive and interpretive exhibits featuring native Kentucky plants and animals. Wonderfully run by the Department of Wildlife and Fishing, they keep it simple but, naturally modern. Begin your viewing with stories told by a Native American girl in the mural called Kentuckians Before Boone. Next, you'll gander at warm-water fish like Bass, Bluegill and Catfish. Around the corner view Kentucky Record Fish mounted on a giant board with storyboards that tell cute tales of the "Big Catch". Have you ever wondered what a bee hive looks like inside, but were afraid to get too close? In the bee tree, you can safely watch honeybees busily at work collecting pollen, feeding their larvae, tending the queen, and communicating to one another using the famous "waggle dance". Two clear plastic tubes allow the bees to come and go from the hive at will, and you can watch them from safety through one of several wildlife viewing windows.

Just around the bend is the most unique site - have you ever seen a live Alligator Snapping Turtle? It was amazing to watch this prehistoric creature perform for us - the combination of claws, scales and turtle shell will catch your attention for sure!

Outdoors in several different, easily accessible areas, take a look at live American Bald Eagles, white-tailed deer with wild turkeys, bison and elk or the new bobcat or black bear exhibit. Further out on the trail is Dragonfly Marsh observation wetland. What can you find?

VEST-LINDSEY HOUSE

401 Wapping Street
(downtown outskirts, near Rebecca-Ruth Candy)

Frankfort 40601

❑ Phone: (502) 564-0900
  http://historicproperties.ky.gov/hp/vlh/Pages/default.aspx
❑ Hours: Monday-Friday 9:00am-4:00pm
❑ Admission: FREE
❑ Tours: no formal tours are offered, just visits and a look around.
❑ Note: State Meeting House for government agencies. You might catch VIP's floating around.

The early 19th century Federal House was the boyhood home of US Senator George Graham Vest. He was a famous trial lawyer, mostly remembered for his "Tribute to the Dog" speech, from which is coined the phrase "dog is man's best friend". He was defending a man whose dog had killed a neighbor's sheep. Of special interest to kids is the floor cloth in the dining areas (vs. carpet). It was the forerunner of linoleum. Also, kids can help demo the dumb-waiter used to serve from the downstairs kitchen. Be sure to pick up a copy of Vest's famous speech before you leave.

HAPPY JACK'S PUMPKIN FARM.

Frankfort. 966 Hickman Hill Road. Pumpkins, petting zoo, u pick produce and corn maze. **Www.happyjackspumpkins.com** (daily each September and October)

CREASEY MAHAN NATURE PRESERVE

12501 Harmony Landing Road (Gene Snyder Freeway exit 9B)

Goshen 40026

❑　　Phone: (502) 228-4362

　　　http://www.creaseymahannaturepreserve.org/

❑　　Nature Center Hours: 10:00am-2:00pm every 3rd Saturday of the
month.

Hike the wooded trails, discover wildlife or just picnic with the family
at this year-round park (open daylight hours). More than 5 miles of
nature trails, 15 minutes to 2 hours in duration, wind through the
preserve. Special places like the Wetlands, the Meadows, the Frog
Pond, and the Rock Platform are favorite "outdoor labs" for students.
The Nature Center highlights lifelike dioramas featuring foxes, deer,
wild turkeys, birds, frogs and some Native American history.

SHAKER VILLAGE

DIXIE BELLE RIVERBOAT

3501 Lexington Road (Shaker Village of Pleasant Hill, US 68E)

Harrodsburg 40330

❑　　Phone: (859) 734-5411 **www.shakervillageky.org**

❑　　Admission: $5.00-$10.00 (age 6+).

❑　　Tours: 2pm and 4pm (April-October).

The 150-passenger riverboat leaves Shaker Landing, the site where
Shakers loaded flatboats with goods headed for Southern markets.
Narrated excursions go through Kentucky River Palisades complete
with limestone canyon, sparkling waterfalls and a close-up of river
flora and fauna.

HARVEST FESTIVAL

Enjoy the autumn's bounty at Shaker Village of Pleasant Hill. Hands-on
harvest activities, including cider pressing and apple butter-making are
a perfect way to greet autumn. Regular admission to Village required
($5-$15). (third weekend in September)

SHAKER CHRISTMAS OPEN HOUSE

Celebrate a simpler, Shaker-style Christmas and discover the spirit of the holidays with seasonal festivities and special programming. Craft store open house with cookies. Music performances. Caroling - evening. Tour admission $3-$7. (first weekend in December)

OLD FORT HARROD STATE PARK

South College Street (US 68, SW of Lexington, near US 127 south)

Harrodsburg 40330

❑   Phone: (859) 734-3314.
http://parks.ky.gov/parks/recreationparks/fort-harrod/default.aspx

❑   Hours: Park open dawn to dusk. Fort: Wednesday-Saturday 9:00am-5:00pm (March - November). Weekdays 8:00am-4:30pm and some weekends (December-February). Museum: Wednesday-Saturday 10:00am-5:00pm. (April-October). Closed winter holidays.

❑   Admission: The park entrance is free. $7.00 adult, $6.00 senior, $4.00 child (6-12) Admission to museum and fort.

❑   Note: Gift Shop, picnicking, animal corral (some petting).

In 1774, Captain James Harrod established the first permanent settlement west of the Alleghenies in the hills of what would become central Kentucky. The reconstructed fort was built near the original. Costumed craftspeople perform pioneer tasks such as broom-making, wood-working, basketry, waving, farming, gardening, blacksmithing and woodworking. The folks even sell their wares in their shops/homes - purchase one as a souvenir. Interact by trying to do some pioneer chores (like dyeing yarn or cooking stew). The most unique spot has to be the frontier schoolhouse. With dirt floors and a pretty schoolteacher you'll learn to use a "hornbook". This is a school slate made of wood with a "laminate" surface made from cow horn chips. The teacher writes the lesson using charcoal and each child holds their "book" in front of them to recite their lessons. And your kids think they have it rough!

FORT HARROD SETTLEMENT & RAID

Old Fort Harrod State Park. This event is a 18th century re-enactment and is their signature event of the year. Presentations, settlers, Natives, sutlers and battles will take place for two short days in the warm June sun just like it did nearly 240 years ago. (third weekend in June)

ABRAHAM LINCOLN BIRTHPLACE NATIONAL HISTORIC SITE

2995 Lincoln Farm Road
(I-65 exit 91, follow KY 61 south to US 31E)

Hodgenville 42748

- ❑   Phone: (270) 358-3137. **www.nps.gov/abli**
- ❑   Hours: Memorial Day-Labor Day 8:00am-6:45pm. Rest of year 8:00am-4:45pm. Closed Thanksgiving, Christmas & New Years. Eastern Time.
- ❑   Admission: Donations.
- ❑   Tours: The Birthplace Unit offers guided walking tours Thursday-Monday between Memorial Day and Labor Day. In the off season tours are self guided.
- ❑   Note: Picnicking, Hiking. A boardwalk ramp trail is available for strollers and wheelchairs. Educators: Abraham Lincoln/Slavery Lesson Plans & Teachers Guides: **www.nps.gov/abli/forteachers/lessonplansandteacherguides.htm**

The Site contains two units located within ten miles of each other: The birthplace unit is a granite memorial with 56 steps, 30 foot wide, leading to the shrine (the steps signify the number of years of Lincoln's life). Enclosed inside are a log cabin and the symbolic birthplace of Abraham Lincoln (1809-1865). The Birthplace Unit also includes the Sinking Spring, the site of the Boundary Oak tree. The Visitor Center houses exhibits on the Lincoln family and a video program on Lincoln's boyhood (humbly produced, as Mr. Lincoln would have wanted it). Our family's highlight was seeing the actual Lincoln family Bible (with study notes written by Lincoln family members)!

LINCOLN'S BIRTHDAY CELEBRATION

Abraham Lincoln Birthplace NHS. The president is honored by a procession to the symbolic birthplace cabin and the placement of a wreath on the door. (on Lincoln's Birthday, Feb. 12)

DID YOU KNOW? Abraham Lincoln had gray eyes.

LINCOLN JAMBOREE

2579 Lincoln Farm Road

Hodgenville 42748

❑ Phone: (270) 358-3545. **www.lincolnjamboree.com**
❑ Shows: Every Saturday night, usually at 8:00pm. Restaurant: Friday, Saturday and Sunday evenings only.
❑ Admission: $10 per person, reserved seating. Meal tickets are $7.99 each.

A well-known country music showplace with family shows since 1954. Country restaurant on premises. A Family Show - Absolutely No Drinking.

LINCOLN MUSEUM

66 Lincoln Square (downtown, town square - look for the bronze Lincoln statue)

Hodgenville 42748

❑ Phone: (270) 358-3163. **www.lincolnmuseum-ky.org**
❑ Hours: Monday-Saturday 8:30am-4:30pm, Sunday 12:30-4:30pm.
❑ Admission: $3.00 adult, $2.50 senior (60+), $1.50 child (5-12).

This two-story museum houses 12 wax figure authentic scenes of great significance in Lincoln's life and our nation's history. The first scene is titled "The Cabin Years" (from local boyhood home) and the last scene #12 is "Ford's Theatre". The 18 minute film shown upstairs is another way to see Lincoln's phases of life. Unlike most wax museums, this one is well lit, not frightening to the younger kids. The scenes are enlightened by the descriptions in the brochure you receive upon paid admission. Well done!

LINCOLN DAYS CELEBRATION

Hodgenville. Honoring native son Abraham Lincoln with a Lincoln Look Alike and Mary Todd Lincoln contests, antique costume contests, pioneer games and rail splitting tournaments. **www.lincolndays.org** (first weekend in October)

LINCOLN'S BOYHOOD HOME

Knob Creek Farm (US 31E northeast)

Hodgenville 42748

- ❏   Phone: (270) 358-3137 **www.nps.gov/abli**
- ❏   Hours: Summers 8:30am-4:30pm, Thursday-Monday.
- ❏   Admission: FREE, donations accepted
- ❏   Note: operated by NPS, affiliated with Abraham Lincoln Birthplace.

"My earliest recollection is of the Knob Creek Place" says Mr. Lincoln. Abraham (at two years old) and his parents and sister Sarah lived here from 1811-1816. Here he learned to talk and later recalled memories of childhood here: a field to pick berries; the baby brother who was born and died here; staying by his mother's side and watching her face while listening to her read her bible; short periods of subscription school (he called it "blab" school because you recited lessons all day long); and falling in the swollen Knob Creek while playing on a footlog. It was here where a young boy Lincoln first saw slaves transported along the road in front of his home. You can take a look inside the cabin and read the giant storyboard. You can also call ahead for a guided tour (school groups get a great study bag to use for further study back home). You'll surely appreciate Abraham's poor beginnings - yet be inspired by the accomplishments of a man who didn't come from affluent means.

BURGOO FESTIVAL

Lawrenceburg. Downtown. A competition and tasting of the stew made with unusual and flavorful ingredients. "Everything but the kitchen sink" is the centerpiece of this tasty festival. **Www.kentuckyburgoo.com** (last long weekend in September)

BELLE OF LOUISVILLE & SPIRIT OF JEFFERSON

(Fourth Street Wharf. I-64 west to Third St. exit, left onto River Rd., right at Second St.)

Louisville 40202

- ❏   Phone: (502) 574-2355 **www.belleoflouisville.org**

❑   Admission: $21.00 adult, $20.00 senior (60+), $12.00 child (3-12).
     Add $11-$20 for lunch or dinner meal added.
❑   Tours: Belle Sightseeing Cruise, (Memorial Day weekend-Labor
     Day). Board at 11:30am or Noon and cruise for two hours shortly after
     that, Tuesday-Sunday. Spirit of Jefferson kid-friendly, historical
     cruises include the Locks Tour (constructed early 1960's, is over 8600
     ft. long and has 9 gates, 22 ft. by 100ft.- best way to see is by boat)
     and the Harbor History most Saturdays.
❑   Note: Both boats have a café, concessions, gift shops and restrooms.
     Besides the major festival cruises listed below, the boats hold special
     cruises for every holiday, including Mothers Day, Fathers Day, Fourth
     of July, Labor Day and Thanksgiving.

The World's Greatest Steamboat was built in 1914 as the "Idlewild"
hauling cargo and people on the Mississippi River. In the mid-1940's
she was renamed "Avalon" and began "tramping" (steamboats used for
traveling from one town to another for business transport and shows).
As the Avalon, she became the most widely traveled steamer in US
history. It is now a National Landmark. Almost 200 feet long and 46
feet wide, she is powered by two steam engines (one port, one
starboard) and has three decks with the capacity to carry 800 people.
The steam calliope, powered by steam from the engine room, has 32
whistles and a sweet Showboat sound. Be sure to check out the
original photos of personnel and similar vessels. While walking thru
the gallery, you'll also be able to chat with the captain and shipmates.
You'll hear talk of the olden days and special points of interest like the
Falls of the Ohio fossil bed, Muhammad Ali center, and famous bridges
and shipyards. Unique to this historical sightseeing tour was the
impressive tie-in of a historical steamboat character sharing stories -
we'd not seen that before! Also, the captain, engineers and 1st mates
were very accessible and happy to sit and spend time answering
questions. NOTE: The narration is key to a good tour. If you can't
hear, move closer to a speaker.

HAPPY EASTER BRUNCH CRUISE. Belle of Louisville. Easter egg
hunts, the Easter Bunny, Brunch Buffet. Admission. (Easter weekend)

THUNDER OVER LOUISVILLE. Belle of Louisville & Spirit of Jefferson. Cruise during the afternoon and stay for the best seats for the fireworks. Admission. (mid-April)

BREAKFAST WITH SANTA & MRS. CLAUSE CRUISE. Spirit of Jefferson. Children will enjoy telling Santa their Christmas wishes, and a photograph that will remind you of this special cruise is included with each reservation. Admission. (mid-December Saturday)

FRAZIER HISTORY MUSEUM

829 West Main Street (i-64 across from Slugger Museum)

Louisville 40202

- ❑ Phone: (502) 459-1247 **www.fraziermuseum.org**
- ❑ Hours: Open throughout the year, except Thanksgiving and Christmas. Monday-Saturday 9:00am-5:00pm, Sunday Noon-5:00pm.
- ❑ Admission: $8-$12 (age 5+).

A boy's dream. The museum encompasses over 800 years of British history and American History from its beginnings through the evolution of armaments. It contains 3 stories of displays, many of which include video footage of reenactments or just further explanation. It is truly fascinating. The best part is that in addition to the exhibits they offer historical interpretations with live actors. We watched a display of "Shakespearian" sword/street fighting complete with quotations of text of Romeo and Juliet. Another was a dramatization of an autobiographical excerpt of a confederate solider at the Battle of Perryville, KY. They offer many others during the day. You can pretty much bet on at least one sword fight demo every visit!

LOUISVILLE BALLET

315 East Main Street (performances at the KY Center for the Arts, 5 Riverfront Plaza)

Louisville 40202

- ❑ Phone: (502) 583-3150 or 584-7777 tickets
  www.louisvilleballet.org

The State Ballet of Kentucky performs classics like "The Nutcracker", "Swan Lake" and many children's classics.

LOUISVILLE SCIENCE CENTER

727 West Main Street (Downtown, I-64 exit 4)

Louisville 40202

❑ Phone: (800) 591-2203. **www.kysciencecenter.org**
❑ Hours: Daily 9:30am-5:00pm (also Friday-Saturday evening until 9:00pm), closed Thanksgiving and Christmas.
❑ Admission: $11.00 - $13.00 adult or child (2-12) (includes admission to science center permanent and traveling exhibits). Combo tickets w/ IMAX theatre approx. $5.00 more per person. $5 after 5pm on Friday and Saturday nights for IMAX film or exhibits.
❑ Note: IMAX Theatre with many daily showtimes. Galaxy Bistro. Educators: guides are found under Teachers/Educator Resources.

As you enter the brightly-colored 40,000 square feet of hands-on science, you might first notice the "Be-in-a-Bubble" or "Bubble Scope" exhibits. Areas covered in the museum include Space Exploration, Egyptian Mummy, Natural History and Health. But, our favorite floor has to be the second floor where "The World We Create" and GROWZONE can be found. GROWZONE is for the younger set (age 7 and under) with their adults. Initially, you may sit back and watch the kiddies play "Splash" (water play) or even "Let's Build" (construction toys, blocks, pulleys and conveyors). However, when you get to "Hop On" or "Take Off" play, the whole family is dressing up and playing pretend. Be a bus, ambulance or plane driver or passenger using apparatus from real vehicles and airplanes. A giant "'Thumbs Up'" to the designers of this giant play equipment! Youngsters can apply what they learned by tagging along with older siblings in the "World We Create" (get an Early Learners Guide from GROWZONE). Now you follow inventions (many created by Kentuckians) like Building Homes, Wind Tunnels, Map Master (find your house), Toppling Towers or Shake, Rattle and Roll (test structures you create with blocks). The World Within Us allows you to tour the human body and check your senses, one at a time. As they say here – "SCIENTISTS AT PLAY"!

LOUISVILLE SLUGGER MUSEUM

800 West Main Street (Eighth and Main, downtown. I-64 West or I-65 South, exit Third Street), **Louisville 40202**

- ❏ Phone: (502) 588-7228. **http://www.sluggermuseum.org**
- ❏ Hours: Monday-Saturday 9:00am-5:00pm, Sunday 11am-5:00pm.
- ❏ Admission $12.00 adult, $11.00 senior (60+) $7.00 child (6-12).
- ❏ Tours: Last Tour begins 1 hour before closing.
- ❏ Note: Be sure to take the tour - everyone gets a small souvenir bat to take home.

You can't miss the entrance to this place. The world's largest baseball bat (120 foot, 68 thousand pounds of steel) rests against the outside wall of the manufacturing plant and the "Let's Play Ball" ball and glove sculpture is the heaviest such structure. Both are great photo ops.

See and touch the actual bats swung by legendary sluggers like Hank

Aaron, Babe Ruth (thicker at the end), Ty Cobb and Ken Griffey, Jr. (lighter). Begin with a video called "The Heart of the Game" that emotionally pays tribute to that magical moment in sports when we hear the crack of the bat. Now that you're in the mood, go through an underground locker room and dugout and onto the field.

LOUISVILLE   SLUGGER   MUSEUM   &   FACTORY   (continued)

After the umpire (guide) explains the rules, he shouts "Play Ball" and the group scatters for pictures, "Chats" with bat boys, and glances at memorabilia from great moments and players. Experience the sensation of a 90 mph pitch coming right at you at the great "Batter Up" famous pitchers display! By the time you've taken another good look at an actual Babe Ruth Home Run bat (see the marks on the bat – each one for a home run!), you'll walk thru a replica Northwest White Ash Forest as you move onto the Hillerich & Bradsby Co. factory.

See modern bats made from a round wooden cylinder.   They are formed from one pass thru a special lathe and then branded with the Louisville Slugger logo and player's name. This is a great All American place for the whole family!

STAGE ONE, THE LOUISVILLE CHILDRENS THEATRE

501 West Main Street (performances at the KY Center for the Arts)

Louisville 40202

❑   Phone: (502) 589-5946 or (800) 989-5946. **www.stageone.org**

For updates visit our website: www.kidslovetravel.com

Their focus is strictly on productions for children and families both at public performances and school outreach programs. Shows like "Huck Finn", "The Velveteen Rabbit", and contemporary Christmas themes like "A Winnie-the-Pooh Christmas" are likely each season. Season runs September-May. Tickets run $15-$20 per show.

THOMAS EDISON HOUSE

729-31 East Washington Street (I-65N to Brook St. exit to Market St., turn right and go east to left on Clay St. to E. Washington St)

Louisville 40202

❑　Phone: (502) 585-5247. **www.historichomes.org**

❑　Hours: Tuesday-Saturday 10:00am-2:00pm. Closed New Years, Derby Day, July 4, Thanksgiving, and Christmas Eve/Day.

❑　Admission: $5.00 adult, $4.00 senior (60+), $3.00 child (6-17).

Although you may think - why take the time to visit a place Edison lived at for only a brief time? Well, we highly recommend you don't have the same regrets as the boss that fired Thomas Edison - the reason he left Louisville. The guides here will highlight many points of the famous inventor's life including working on the railroad, learning Morse Code (try it yourself in his room) to being fired and turning out his first invention, the stock ticker. A great video describes the inventor's life. Did you know he actually started General Electric? Some of his 1093 patents are on display including: early motion pictures (the first one was of a man sneezing!), phonograph, dictating machines, and a collection of electric light bulbs. They have cute light bulb souvenirs to chose from and a picture of our favorite invention - the Power Nap! You have to go just to get the scoop on that!

EDISON BIRTHDAY PARTY Edison's Home. Celebrate Thomas Edison's birthday with a visit to his Butchertown home full of artifacts and tales of little known facts. FREE. (first or second Saturday in February).

CHRISTMAS OPEN HOUSE Edison's Home. Holiday decorations, music, refreshments. Admission. (first Saturday in December)

LOUISVILLE STONEWARE COMPANY

731 Brent Street (I-65 off Broadway Street exit east to Barret Street, turn right), **Louisville 40204**

- ❑   Phone: (502) 582-1900 **www.louisvillestoneware.com**
- ❑   Hours: Monday-Saturday 10am-5pm
- ❑   Admission: $8.00 adult, $7.00 senior, $6 child (6-18).
- ❑   Tours: Monday-Friday at 10:30am and 1:30pm. 35-40 minutes. Call ahead for best secure spots.
- ❑   Note: Paint your own pottery workshop - pay by the item - excellent way to end tour (make pre-arrangements with 5 or more).

Nationally famous hand-painted pottery (dinnerware, ovenware, giftware) since 1879. On tour, see the entire process. Begin at the Raw Clay Storage Bin where mounds of dry clay are stacked as tall as your garage. They next mix raw clay with water, take out air bubbles and finally extrude clay fit for the potter's wheel. Unusually shaped pieces (like birdhouses) are cast upstairs. You'll see the jigger production pieces created on a potters wheel with molds and the potter's special trained touch. The handles are all hand formed by two quiet, artistic women. There's a large room full of women painting trains, fish, Noah's Ark, etc. on the wares. You next see the pieces dipped and set to dry in kilns. Note: We think the best souvenirs of all are those hand-made, especially by your kids. For around $15-$20 your kids can create their own design on pottery made here. What a wonderful way to have kids apply what they just saw being made to their own creation!

AMERICAN PRINTING HOUSE FOR THE BLIND

1839 Frankfort Avenue (I-64 and US 42 east)

Louisville 40206

- ❑ Phone: (502) 895-2405 or (800) 223-1839. **www.aph.org**
- ❑ Hours: Museum: Monday-Friday 8:30am-4:30pm. Saturday 10:00am-3:00pm. Closed holidays and Derby Day.
- ❑ Admission: FREE
- ❑ Tours: Monday-Thursday at 10:00am and 2:00pm. Make reservations for groups of 10 or more. Suggested age for touring is age 9 years and up. Tour takes one hour.
- ❑ Educators: click on the k12 school groups - bottom of page facts about Braille, dog guides, meeting blind people, etc.

Browse through a Braille magazine as you wait for your tour to begin. Founded in 1858, this place is one of the world's largest and oldest printing companies creating products for the visually-impaired. You'll start in the hands-on area (our favorite part - truly fascinating - really!) where visitors can actually learn some of the Braille alphabet, read a popular book in both Braille and written word, or test a talking color analyzer that helps the color-blind match their clothing. Try your math skills with multiplication cards for the blind. Next, briefly tour the plant where they print, bind and proofread all kinds of books and magazines. The museum displays embossed books, early mechanical Braille writers and tactile maps and globes. This is also where you take home a hand-made souvenir of you name typed in Braille. A truly curious, enchanting place! Could you guess what would possibly be their largest Braille project ever? - The World Book Encyclopedia - 145 volumes (see it!).

HADLEY POTTERY

1570 Story Avenue
(halfway between Amer. Printing & Edison's Home)

Louisville 40206

- ❑ Phone: (502) 584-2171. **www.hadleypottery.com**
- ❑ Hours: Store hours are Monday-Friday from 8:30am-5:00pm. Eastern time and Saturday from 9:00am-1:00pm. Saturday hours are extended from the second week in November until Christmas.

- ❑ Admission: FREE
- ❑ Tours: Monday-Thursday at 2:00pm (except in the summer when the temp. is over 85 degrees). No age restrictions; however, small children and elderly or handicapped will not be able to easily manage the very steep staircase to the basement where most of the activity occurs. Some young children feel the basement is also dark and scary.

Pottery by Mary Alice Hadley has an international reputation and is known for its whimsical designs of clay stoneware. They use a process (you will see during the tour) called "underglaze decoration". The pottery is fired only one time; and this single fire process produces ware with a maximum bond between the body, decoration and glaze, with the result that the decoration is as permanent as the piece. In ware produced by the alternate process of separate firings for the body, glaze and decoration (as is the practice with most dinnerware), the decoration (and sometimes the glaze) is readily subject to abrasion and the chemical action of strong cleaning solutions and to crazing. The high temperature limits the range of colors that can be used in applying decoration. Colors adaptable for use with the white over-glaze are blue, green and rust, with blue-black and yellow available under special circumstances. You'll see artisans hand-painting with these colors on the second floor. Most children like the painting area best.

LOCUST GROVE HISTORIC HOME

561 Blankenbaker Lane (I-264 exit 22, US 42 west or I-71 exit 2, follow signs), **Louisville 40207**

- ❑ Phone: (502) 897-9845.

www.locustgrove.org

- ❑ Hours: Monday-Saturday 10:00am-4:30pm, Sunday 1:30-4:30pm. Hands-on History open Tuesday-Saturday 11:00am-3:00pm, June-August. Closed New Years, Easter, Derby Day, Thanksgiving, Christmas, and January.
- ❑ Admission: $8.00 adult, $7.00 senior (60+), $4.00 child (6-12).

- ❑ Tours: start each hour on the quarter hours - last one at 3:15pm.
- ❑ Note: Pioneer Days or Woodworking Camp available in summer. Gift Shop. Video about history of site shown in visitor's center. Educators: Teachers Packets **www.locustgrove.org/locustgrovepacket.pdf**

The retirement home (beginning in 1809) of George Rogers Clark - a frontiersman and Revolutionary War General. The mansion, garden and nine outbuildings are furnished in period. Start in the parlor room where such guests as Presidents James Monroe, Zachary Taylor or Andrew Jackson were greeted. Also Lewis & Clark (William) visited and stored artifacts from exhibitions in the ballroom upstairs. In the Dining Room, you'll find out why sugar was kept in large cabinets under lock & key. Why was the letter "J" missing from the alphabet in pioneer days? Did you know settlers (pre Civil War) wore shoes with no left or right foot distinction?

The Hands-On History Cabin is highly recommended (summer only). This log cabin is where children can try on clothing reproductions and sort through the contents of a Revolutionary War soldier's trunk. Kids can also try quilting, weaving, pioneer games, carding wool, surveying and mapping a new city or writing with a real quill pen. Photos in this area make wonderful souvenirs - great learning too. And, while you're out there, take a peak at what Slave Life was like in the new exhibit building.

KENTUCKY DERBY MUSEUM AND CHURCHILL DOWNS

704 Central Avenue (I-264 & Taylor Blvd., Follow signs)

Louisville 40208

- ❑ Phone: (502) 637-1111or (502) 637-7097 **www.derbymuseum.org**
- ❑ Hours: Monday-Saturday 9:00am-5:00pm, Sunday, 11:00am-5:00pm. Opens at 8am summer Monday-Saturday. Closed Oaks and Derby days (first Friday/Sat. in May), Thanksgiving and Christmas.
- ❑ Admission: $15.00 adult, $14.00 senior (60+), 76.00 child (5-14) includes Historic walking tour of Churchill Downs.
- ❑ Tours: Finish Line Shop, Derby Café (lunch).

Although the actual Derby Day and Churchill Downs races may not be appropriate for the young kids, the Museum and Tour of Churchill Downs is fun for the family.

The museum has 3 floors of displays that showcase thoroughbred racing in the Derby - the greatest two minutes in sports. Different areas focus on: The Horses (owners and trainers, too), The Jockeys and Derby Day. The 360 degree audiovisual recreation is a must see. Located in the center of the first floor, the circular theatre really captures the "feeling" of all people involved. Other highlights are the Starting Gate (you walk thru one as you enter the museum); "Weigh in Please" exhibit where you weigh yourself the day of the race and compare your weight to an average jockey (they average 126 pounds). Finally, our favorite, "Riders Up" - try riding like a jockey on a horse in position to win the race. Don't sit down on the saddle - you'll lose the race! Oh, and look for the Derby hat contest exhibit – quite a show.

SPEED ART MUSEUM

2035 South Third Street (exit I-65 to St. Catherine, Arthur St. or Eastern Parkway - adjacent to the Univ. of Louisville)

Louisville 40208

❑   Phone: (502) 634-2700. **www.speedmuseum.org**

❑   Hours: Wednesday-Saturday 10:00am-5:00pm and Sunday Noon-5:00pm. Later on Fridays, too.

❑   Admission:$10 adult, $8 senior (65+), $5 child (3-17). Enjoy FREE admission to the Museum's permanent collection & Art Sparks Interactive Family gallery on First Friday of the month from 5 to 9.

Although a planned group tour of any significant art museum is a wonderful cultural experience for children, the Art Sparks Interactive Gallery inside this museum makes this art museum the best for kids. Don a Dutch collar and cape and play Rembrandt, dance inside video artwork, design your own room furniture, or turn your picture into pop art

(Daddy looked like a monster!). In the Electronic Art Room, young visitors can create digital art while visiting museums around the world via the Internet. Explore the Native American Collection and sit in a see-thru teepee, do a "breeze of blessing dance" inside an Egungan costume from West African Vistas, Invent a story and then make it come true in the Shadow Play super projector, Planet Preschool is a whole room of textures, shapes and colors AND you get to TOUCH EVERYTHING. Most stations engage for at least 10 minutes. Older kids actually learn principles of art.

If you venture, as a family, into the "grown-up" galleries be sure to get a Gallery Pack, a kid-size bag filled with puzzles, seek-and-find, and other hand-outs that take "boring" out of the kid's vocabulary.

HILTON GARDEN INN LOUISVILLE AIRPORT

2735 Crittenden Drive (I-65 south take Crittenden Drive exit)

Louisville 40209

❑   Phone: (502) 637-2424   **www.hiltongardeninn.com**

If you plan to spend the night and go to several attractions near the airport, overnight where there's a shuttle to the airport and most every major Louisville attraction is only a few exits away. Each room is spacious enough with added amenities like a refrigerator and microwave. They have an indoor swimming pool with a hot tub and workout center.

PORTLAND MUSEUM

2308 Portland Avenue

Louisville 40212

❑   Phone: (502) 776-7678 **www.goportland.org**
❑   Hours: Tuesday-Thursday 10:00am-4:30pm
❑   Admission: $5-$7.00 (age 6+).

Do newsreels of the 1937 flood or a terrain model of the Falls of the Ohio fossil bed interest you? Study 19th century times (when the town was a thriving river port) through dioramas and mannequins titled "Portland: the Land, the River and the People". The museum is housed in Beech Grove, built in 1852 as a country estate. It also features a 23 minute historical light & sound show.

LOUISVILLE ZOO

1100 Trevilian Way (I-264 exit 14)

Louisville 40213

- ❑ Phone: (502) 459-2181. **www.louisvillezoo.org**
- ❑ Hours: Daily 10:00am-5:00pm (April-Labor Day); open 'til 4:00pm rest of year. Closed New Years, Thanksgiving and Christmas. Last entrance is one hour before closing.
- ❑ Admission: $14.95 adult, $10.50 senior (60+) and child (3-11). 4d theater, rides and special exhibits extra. Reduced winter rates.
- ❑ Note: Mini-train ride circling zoo. Picnicking spots. Cafes. Carousel rides. Raorchestra - summertime Louisville orchestra concert series on the lawn. 4-D Ride Theatre.

The Mammal and bird exhibits here are arranged by geographic regions. One of the largest arachnid (spiders, centipedes) exhibits is here and it's the only one like it in the U.S. The Islands Pavilion, Indonesian Village is home to tigers and orangutans; there's a walk-thru aviary; the Aquarium has a rainforest, reptiles and fish; the petting zoo features African farm animals; and the MetaZoo Education Center provides amphibian exhibits and microscopes through which small creatures can be viewed. The Gorilla Forest and the Australian Outback include a lot of close looks back from the animals. Cold blooded mammals find their haven in Glacier Run. This is where you'll find the polar and grizzly bears.

MEGACAVERNS

A constant 60 degrees underground, the Louisville Mega Cavern (**http://www.louisvillemegacavern.com**) is a perfect activity for a rainy or sweltering summer day. You'll discover a guided tram tour rich in history, geology, mining and recycling.

For the adventuresome, glide behind a certified tour guide on the 2-hour underground MEGA Zips. Featuring six underground zip lines, including a fun filled dual racing zip, three awesome challenge bridges that will test your skill, balance, and mettle; this tour is guaranteed to get your heart racing and your adrenaline pumping. The tour path leads you into never before seen sections of the manmade cavern. This is the only underground zipline in the country!

For those who want a more relaxing adventure, be sure to take our one hour Historic Tram Tour through part of 17 miles of man-made passageways beneath the City of Louisville. Learn about the early limestone mining operations that created the caverns, dioramas to explain how the cavern could have been used as a fallout shelter, and even a little on the recycling that goes on below ground…even growing worms! Because you ride through the cavern and never walk, this tour is especially convenient for children of all ages, seniors, and the physically challenged.

Tip: Weight guidelines are 55 to 275 pounds. Children up to 15 years old must be accompanied by an adult. Zips run $59-$79 for a zip tour.

FIRES GLASS BLOWING GALLERY

170 Carter Avenue (I-65 exit 121 E to Bluelick Road North to Carter Avenue)

Louisville 40229

- ❑ Phone: (502) 955-1010
- ❑ Hours: Monday-Saturday 10:00am-5:00pm.
- ❑ Admission: FREE
- ❑ Tours: Daily, groups must have appointments. Best to call ahead for best viewing times each week.
- ❑ Note: Café - lunch at glass counters along the large glass blower observation windows.

Tour this facility and watch artists create small and large unusually shaped glass blown art. Although the thought of gift glass art may not appeal to parents with young children (to display in their home), the idea of purchases as gifts will certainly appeal to you more after watching something being created. Try to figure out which shape they're forming before they finish (there's a good chance it may be something with fins or feathers).

LOUISVILLE RIVER BATS

401 East Main Street (Louisville Slugger Field)

Louisville 40233

- ❑ Phone: (502) 367-9121. **www.batsbaseball.com**
- ❑ Season: April-September

Since Louisville is all about Bats, watch the BATS in action. The Louisville River Bats meet their opponents at home in Louisville Slugger Field (downtown near cross-section of the itnerstates and the river). What amusement, entertainment, prizes and good, old-fashioned fun! Look for mascot Buddy the Bat, or ride the carousel, buy some Cracker Jack and then dance along with comical crew and their between-innings antics. We had so much fun eating and tasting (reasonably priced tickets and food) Americana baseball. AAA professional baseball farm club for the Cincinnati Reds. Tickets run $6.00-$10.00.

TOM SAWYER, E.P. STATE PARK

3000 Freys Hill Road (Gene Snyder Freeway northeast to westbound Westport Road exit)

Louisville 40241

❑   Phone: (502) 426-8950

http://www.parks.ky.gov/parks/recreationparks/tom-sawyer/

Best known for the following unique amenities: an archery park, a radio controlled airfield, a summer aquatics program, the bicycle motto-cross track or indoor team sports in the park's gymnasium. There's also a few miles of hiking trails…a fav is the 1.25 mile Goose Creek nature trail.

KENTUCKY DERBY FESTIVAL

The celebration of all things Kentucky & the Derby. (800) 928-FEST. www.kdf.org. (mid-April thru first Saturday in May)

THUNDER OVER LOUISVILLE, riverfront. The nation's largest fireworks and pyrotechnics display on earth (1 million people)! Also a great military air show. (mid-April Saturday)

GREAT BALLOON RACE, Kentucky Fair and Exposition Center. Over 35 hot air balloons in the chase of the "hare" balloon. (last Saturday in April)

BEDLAM IN THE STREETS BED RACES, Louisville Motor Speedway. Evening bed races. Corporate teams race in themed beds. Parade of beds at 6pm. (first Monday in May)

GREAT STEAMBOAT RACE, riverfront. The race between the Belle of Louisville against a rival boat like the Delta Queen.

PEGASUS PARADE, downtown. Spectacle of colorful floats, marching bands, giant inflatables, equestrians and celebrities starting west on Broadway. (first Thursday in May)

GOVERNOR'S DERBY BREAKFAST, Capitol grounds, Frankfort. (800) 960-7200. Everyone is invited to the Capitol building for a free breakfast along with entertainment and crafts to enjoy afterwards. (morning of the 1st Saturday in May - Derby Day)

WATERFRONT INDEPENDENCE FESTIVAL

www.louisvillewaterfront.com Live music, a RiverBats baseball game, children's activities, festival food and fireworks extravaganza. Star of Louisville Fireworks Cruises. (around July 4th)

KENTUCKY STATE FAIR

11 days of fun filled activities and events for the whole family. Enjoy exhibits, crafts, animals and contests at America's largest air-conditioned fair. The Thrillway excitement returns for the adventurous ones, music's hottest stars will electrify Freedom Hall and Cardinal Stadium, while the splendor of the World's Championship Horse Show will take your breath away. **Www.kystatefair.org** Admission. (starts mid-August for 11 days)

FESTIVAL OF TREES & LIGHTS

Slugger Field. (502) 629-kids. The switch is thrown at dusk (~7:40pm) to illuminate downtown with over 40 buildings covered in holiday lights. There's also Santa's arrival, fireworks, a global village, entertainment throughout the day, and a children's holiday parade in the daytime. Brunch with Santa & Animals at the Zoo runs weekends in December. Admission, ticketed events. **www.facebook.com/KosairChildrens** (mid-November weekend)

BERNHEIM FOREST

KY 245 (I-65 exit 112)

Louisville (Clermont) 40110

- ❑ Phone: (502) 955-8512 **http://www.bernheim.org**
- ❑ Hours: Center, Daily 9:00am-5:00pm. Park, 7:00am to sunset. Closed Christmas and New Year's.

❑   Admission: Only charged Saturday, Sunday & Holidays. $5.00 per vehicle.
❑   Note: biking and geocaching paths.

The official state arboretum with 2000 plants identified, a 12,000 acre forest, 30 miles of hiking trails, and a fishing lake and visitors center. Take the auto tour of sculpture (we liked "Emerging", with its "pockets" of peeping holes) or stop in the Birds of Prey Building or Live Deer Pen. Get a Scavenger Hunt list before you hit the trails. There's a café and a visitors center, too.

COLORFEST Bernheim Forest. **www.bernheim.org/colorfest.htm** Fall festival featuring craft and nature exhibits for children, food, storytelling, music and activities. Hay Maze, paint pumpkins, puppet shows and hayrides. Admission per vehicle. (third weekend in October)

JEFFERSON MEMORIAL FOREST

11311 Mitchell Hill Road
(I-265 exit 8, southern edge of Jefferson County)

Louisville (Fairdale) 40118

❑   Phone: (502) 368-5404. **www.memorialforest.com**
❑   Hours: Dawn to dusk
❑   Admission: FREE

The forest is a woodland tribute to the area citizens who served in the nation's wars. Dedicated as a National Audubon Wildlife Sanctuary, the land has over 5000 acres of forest with streams, birds and wildlife, steep slopes of second growth woods of pine, oak and chestnut. Recreation areas, nature trails and a welcome center serve as starting points for nature walks and star-gazing programs. The easiest and shortest trail for young families is the Tulip Tree Trail (paved 0.2 miles, one way).

KENTUCKY RAILWAY MUSEUM

136 South Main Street (BG Parkway exit 10; SRKY 52 or US 31E between Bardstown & Hodgenville)

New Haven 40051

❑   Phone: (502) 549-5470 or **http://www.kyrail.org**

❑   Hours: Museum: Monday-Saturday 10:00am-4:00pm, Sunday 1:00-
     4:00pm (April-December). Rail Ride: Weekends (April -mid
     December). Tuesdays, too (May-September). Departures at 11:00am
     1:00pm & 2:00pm depending on weekend.

❑   Admission: Museum only: $5.00 adult, $2.00 child (3-12). Train ticket
     (includes museum): $18.00 adult, 13.00 child (2-12). Higher fares for
     Steam Weekends & Locomotive Cab Rides (ride with the engineers).

❑   Note: Museum Gift Shop with lots of railroad-themed items. Events
     including train robberies, pizza Train and special holiday train rides.
     Call ahead to see if "Thomas the Tank Engine" is visiting this year
     (usually mid-summer)!

Ride through a scenic and historic Rolling Fork River Valley. Pass
woodlands, farmlands and small communities. Learn about the engine
and coaches you are riding on. The 22 mile, 1 ½ hour journey is
powered by steam or diesel locomotive carrying authentic coaches on
the rails. The museum houses a collection of artifacts and memorabilia
in a replica of the original New Haven depot. The kids love the
sleeping car exhibit, serving cart, railway post office and track bicycle
inspection car. You can also watch several different toy train layouts
operate in the model train center.   Also see some layouts under
construction. The train ride is smooth - parents could bring a magazine
and the kids maybe an activity book. A Railway Coloring Book (given
to each child on the trip back) is a fun souvenir (be sure to bring your
own crayons).

SANTA EXPRESS Kentucky Railway Museum. Train Rides with
Santa and treats. Admission. (first weekend in December and every
weekend until Christmas)

KENTUCKY SPEEDWAY

(I-71 exit 57 or 55, follow signs)

Sparta 41095

❑   Phone: (859) 647-43   **http://www.kentuckyspeedway.com**

A 1.5 mile tri-oval, state-of-the-art NASCAR track that opened the
summer of 2000. Call or visit website for racing schedule.

LINCOLN HOMESTEAD STATE PARK

5079 Lincoln Park Road (BG Parkway to US 150 east or SRKY 555 south. On SRKY 528 and 438)

Springfield 40069

❑ Phone: (859) 336-7461.
   http://parks.ky.gov/parks/recreationparks/lincoln-homestead/
❑ Hours: Park - dawn to dusk. Museum: Daily 8:00am-6:00pm (May-September).
❑ Admission to Museum: $1.50-$2.00 (age 6+).
❑ Note: Gift shop, picnicking.

The Berry Home - Nancy Hanks lived in this home when she was courted by Thomas Lincoln. In the huge living room before the immense fireplace, Thomas proposed to Nancy. A copy of their marriage bond hangs there. In the knolls near the Beech Fork River, the buildings are filled with pioneer furniture. The buildings on site are replicas of the 1782 cabin and blacksmith shop where Lincoln's father was reared and learned his trade. It was also the home of Mordecai Lincoln, a favorite uncle of the President. Lincoln Homestead also has a shelter house and playground within walking distance of the cabins.

KENTUCKY CROSSROADS HARVEST FESTIVAL

A fall harvest festival with agricultural products and farmers featured in areas of craft, food, and contests. **www.kyharvestfestival.com** (early October weekend)

TAYLORSVILLE LAKE STATE PARK

PO Box 205 (I-64 exit 32, take KY 55 south to KY 44/KY 248 east)

Taylorsville 40071

❑ Phone: (502) 477-8713 or (502) 477-8766 marina
   http://parks.ky.gov/parks/recreationparks/taylorsville-lake/
❑ Educators: Education Center web stories, lessons and games about the dam are found here: **http://education.usace.army.mil/index.cfm**

This park boasts a new campground perfect for the numerous fishermen or equestrians that love the fishing and horse trails through forested countryside. The Visitor's Center (KY 2239) is a pioneer homestead and the Dam Visitor's Center and Overlook has a theatre and trail to the historic homestead. There's also a marina and boat rentals.

MUSIC RANCH USA

407 South Street (off Hwy 31W)

West Point 40177

- ❑ Phone: (502) 922-9393.
- ❑ Hours: Show every Saturday at 7:30pm. Other music shows vary.
- ❑ Admission: $10.00 adult, $5.00 child (3-11).
- ❑ Miscellaneous: Chow hall adjacent, open 5:30pm - midnight.

Country jamboree with old time rock, blues, some Bluegrass and gospel.

TOWNEPLACE SUITES BY MARRIOTT LOUISVILLE NORTH

703 North Shore Drive, Jeffersonville IN 67130. www.marriott.com (just over the Ohio River on the I-65 or 2nd Street Bridge). Lodging starts around $116/night.

TownePlace Suites Louisville North is the go-to choice among extended-stay Louisville hotels in Jeffersonville. Our beautiful townhouse community is located just 1 mile from downtown and the KFC Yum Center, home to the University of Louisville Cardinals, and walking distance from excellent dining along the Ohio River. Whether searching hotels in Jeffersonville / Louisville for business or leisure, they'll get you where you're going in minutes: Riverfront, Kentucky Fair & Expo Center, KY Derby Center, Louisville Slugger and more. Their extended-stay Louisville suites and studios feature fully equipped kitchens, large work spaces and free high-speed wireless Internet. More than a place to stay, the Jeffersonville, IN hotel is a true home-away-from-home, complete with outdoor pool, BBQ area with gas grills, coin laundry and fitness room.

Chapter 2
Area - North East (NE)

Our Favorites...

* Candy Factories - Lexington Area

* Kentucky Horse Park - Lexington

* Lexington Children's Museum - Lexington

* Kentucky Folk Art Center - Morehead

* Newport Aquarium - Newport

* Carter Caves State Resort Park - Olive Hill

* Daniel Boone National Forest - Winchester

* Big Bone Lick State Park - Union

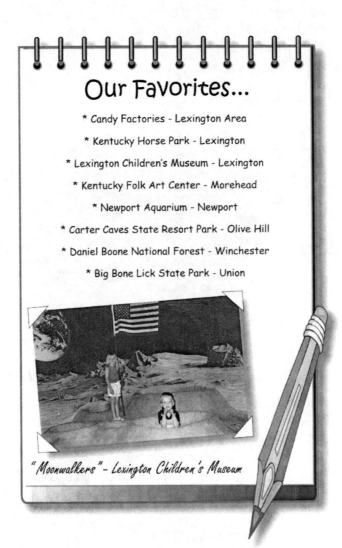

"Moonwalkers" - Lexington Children's Museum

I-75 Corridor

We'll begin in Northern Kentucky, just over the border from Cincinnati, Ohio. Just a few miles east of Covington are the now bustling city of Newport. Many are familiar with the oceanic adventures at Newport Aquarium. If you haven't visited recently, we've heard the sharks have been waiting for you! Not to mention, the penguins, the pirates, and the elegant jelly fish. The new and expanding Levee Complex has fun shopping and dining nearby.

Back on I-75 heading south (exit 175) you won't want to miss Big Bone Lick State Park. This is the birthplace of American Vertebrate Paleontology...the greatest ice age graveyard ever found (herds of giant mastodons, mammoths, and bison came to the warm salt springs)! Erosion may still reveal bones (look for them while hiking), especially along the creek. A museum with video presentations describes the area. A live buffalo herd now roams the property and your kids can touch Mastodon teeth!

Let's move on to Lexington factory tours of Toyota (by tram) or Old Kentucky Candies or Ruth Hunt Candies (by foot). UK chocolates are for the loyal fans. Visit the actual UK campus for a stop at the Webb Museum of Anthropology or a walk through Arboretum Park. "A Walk Across Kentucky" showcases vegetation grouped by region. Whimsical "garden art" is found at the Children's Garden. Be sure to get a colorful map and have fun playing the Garden Game.

While the older kids may spend hours, even days, at the Kentucky Horse Park (our favorite area is the Parade of Breeds), the younger set will fall in love with the Lexington Children's Museum. Hands-on exhibits cover science (a talking brain or walk-thru heart), nature (make a quake, create soil wars), world geography and culture. While you're downtown, stop by Thoroughbred Park on Main Street where 7 life-sized bronze statues of horses racing are climbable and great photo-ops!

Now, let's get into the spirit of frontiersmen. Fort Boonesborough State Park is a recreated village near Winchester that served as a fortress, stopping point and trade center. Begin your visit watching a film showing the struggles of the fort, especially withstanding a

nine-day attack by Indians and Frenchmen. Within the fort's
walls, resident artisans share pioneer experiences and demonstrate
crafts such as pottery, candle-making, weaving and cooking.

Head farther east to the town of Morehead for a taste of
Appalachia. Beginning with the education of Appalachian peoples
at Morehead State University, see how graduates and others living
in the state created famous folk art (KY Folk Art Center). Watch
the "World of Wonder" video, then look throughout the gallery for
recycled material sculpted into famous shapes like Uncle Sam or
George Washington. A favorite is "Precious Memories"- a
monkey made with junk – can you find the cow and chess piece?
Before you leave town, check out the Minor Clark State Fish
Hatchery. Here, fish are produced in over 100 ponds with racers
(give the fish a chance to exercise).

A QUICK GLANCE AT THIS AREA...

Ashland
- Highlands Museum
- Summer Motion
- Winter Wonderland of Lights
- Country Music Hwy

Burlington
- Dinsmore Homestead

Covington
- Totters Otterville
- Behringer/Crawford Museum
- Mainstrasse Village
- Railway Expo Museum

Falmouth
- Kincaid Lake St Pk
- Kentucky Wool Festival

Greenup
- Greenbo Lake St Resort Pk

Lexington
- Ashland, Henry Clay
- Old Ky Candies
- McConnell Springs
- Parkette Drive –in
- Univ of Ky
- Lexington Children's Theatre
- Lexington Legends Baseball
- Lexington Philharmonic
- Explorium of Lexington
- Hunt-Morgan House
- Mary Todd Lincoln home
- Ky Horse Park

Lexington (continued)
- Waveland St Historic Pk
- Raven Run Nature Sanctuary
- Aviation Museum of Ky
- Keeneland Track Kitchen
- Toyota Motor Manuf Ky tour
- Ruth Hunt Candies
- Bluegrass State Games

Louisa
- Yatesville Lake St Pk

Maysville
- Maysville Floodwall Murals
- Natl Undergrd Railroad Museum
- Pumpkinfest

Morehead
- Ky Folk Art Ctr
- Minor Clark Fish Hatchery
- Morehead St Univ
- Cave Run Storytelling Festival
- Blue Licks Battlefield

Newport
- Newport Aquarium
- Ride the Ducks
- World Peace Bell
- BB Riverboats

Nicholasville
- Jim Beam Nature Preserve
- Sally Brown Nature Preserve
- Camp Nelson
- Harry Miller Lock Collection

Olive Hill
- Carter Caves St Pk
- Grayson Lake St Pk

Petersburg
- Creation Museum

Union
- Big Bone Lick St Pk

Versailles
- Bluegrass Scenic RR
- Jouett House
- Nostalgia Station

Washington
- Harriet Beecher Stowe home

West Liberty
- Sorghum Fest

Winchester
- Daniel Boone Natl Forest

HIGHLANDS MUSEUM & DISCOVERY CENTER

1620 Winchester Avenue (I-64 to US 23 right into town)

Ashland 41105

- ❑ Phone: (606) 329-8888. **www.highlandsmuseum.com**
- ❑ Hours: Wednesday-Friday 10:00am-4:00pm, Saturday 10am-6pm. Closed New Years, July 4, Thanksgiving and Christmastime.
- ❑ Admission: $5.00-$6.50 per person (age 2+).
- ❑ Note: also Star Lab Planetarium shows.

The Country music exhibit features the Judds and other famous Appalachian entertainers... but there's a lot more to look at in the Children's Discovery Center. Also see displays on Appalachian culture, Native American artifacts, and industrial heritage of the area, antique clothing and a "Granny" Toothman spinner/weaver. Interactive areas change twice a year. Look for hands-on exhibits about pioneer exploring, air flight, Hannah Montana artifacts (Billy Ray was from around here) or life on the river. Youth and adults can leave the river and explore a cave. Discovery Cavern is a walk-thru, crawl through cave where bats fly and rock formations stand tall. Even find some rock art. They purpose to make every "zone" interactive for kids.

SUMMER MOTION

Ashland. Central Park & Riverfront. 4th of July five day celebration is a huge party with fireworks, concerts (top name entertainment), food, etc. **http://summermotion.com** (first five days of July)

WINTER WONDERLAND OF LIGHTS

www.winterwonderlandoflights.com Ashland. Central Park. 700,000 plus lights of 35 displays seen by carriage ride through community with centerpiece at Central Park. Also activity at Highland Museum & Festival of Trees., train rides (fee for rides). FREE (mid-November thru New Years Eve)

COUNTRY MUSIC HIGHWAY 23

(Maps available in downtown Ashland or downtown Paintsville)

Ashland / Paintsville 41105

❑   Phone: (800) 542-5790

US 23 in Kentucky is a tribute to Eastern Kentucky country music stars including The Judds, Tom T. Hall, Billy Ray Cyrus, Ricky Skaggs, and Patty Loveless. In Ashland, stop for a bite at the Country Music Hwy. Café. Butcher Hollow is the birthplace of Loretta Lynn "The Coal Miner's Daughter" and her sister, Crystal Gayle. Located seven miles from downtown Paintsville, souvenirs of Loretta and Crystal are available at the No. 5 General Store owned by their brother Herman Webb. Herman will give you a personal tour of the home (for $5.00 per person), still furnished as it was years ago. Loretta and family memorabilia is scattered throughout. Any country music fan will want to say they visited. SRKY 321 and SRKY 1107 north to SRKY 302 east, then follow signs off Miller's Creek.

DINSMORE HOMESTEAD

5656 Burlington Pike (I-75/71 exit 181 to KY 18 west)

Burlington 41005

❑   Phone: (859) 586-6117. **www.dinsmorefarm.org**
❑   Hours: Wednesday, Saturday, Sunday 1:00-5:00pm (April thru mid-December). Last tour leaves at 4:00pm.
❑   Admission: $5.00 adult, $3.00 senior (60+), $2.00 student (5-17).
❑   FREEBIES: Biographies of the folks that lived here throughout history are online. Might want to check it out on your laptop before or after a visit.

What is The Dinsmore Homestead? The Dinsmore Homestead is a unique historic site where visitors can learn what rural life was like in the 19th and early 20th centuries. Nature enthusiasts enjoy the hiking trails developed in cooperation with the Kentucky Nature Conservancy and County Parks Department. Kids can relieve boredom by experiencing a historical place both inside and outside - where they can run about and explore their own way. This Living History Farm, with a museum and nature center on the farm, was the property of the Dinsmore family who originally came from the Deep South.   Learn of their benevolent treatment of slaves. Discovery Days or School Living History (hands-on) Tours are your best bet to take advantage of this facility (usually weekends).

CHRISTMAS IN THE COUNTRY Dinsmore Farm. Open house with holiday decorations, music and refreshments served. Admission. (first long full weekend in December)

CHRISTMAS DOWN ON THE FARM

Mullins Log Cabin. (859) 824-0565. An old-fashioned country gathering with craft demos and wagon rides and warm food. (first weekend in December)

TOTTER'S OTTERVILLE @ JOHNNY'S TOYS

4314 Boron Drive (I-75 exit 185 to I-275 exit 79, Taylor Mill/Covington exit. Head north, at fourth traffic light, turn left)

Covington 41015

- ❑ Phone: (859) 491-1441. **www.johnnystoys.com**
- ❑ Hours: Monday-Saturday 10:00am-5:00pm. Friday-Saturday open until 8:00pm. Sunday 11:00am-5:00pm. Holiday schedule varies - see website.
- ❑ Admission: $8.95 child (ages 9 months up to 10 years). Adults FREE.
- ❑ Note: Totter's Otterville is inside Johnny's Toys. A café is on the premises with many common kiddie foods like pizza, hot dogs, nuggets but also wraps & subs and snacks. They do not fry anything here - all baked.

As you enter Johnny's Toys, you'll notice lots of color, lots of toys and so many trains. Kids can begin by playing at the train tables scattered in the store. After paying admission, young families can enter Totter's Otterville. Here, even more trains, a mini toy section with toy animals and dollhouses, a ball pit or climbing zone, a water play area, and a pretend play area with dress up clothes and props. In the seasonal outdoor area, kids can play on a gym structure, dig for dino bones, ride a mini trolley or try to solve the walk-thru maze.

BEHRINGER / CRAWFORD MUSEUM

1600 Montague Road (I-75, exit either 5th Street or 12th Street/Pike Street, follow signs to Devou Park)

Covington 41011

- ❑ Phone: (859) 491-4003 **www.bcmuseum.org**
- ❑ Hours: Tuesday-Saturday 10:00am-5:00pm, Sunday 1:00-5:00pm. Closed holidays.
- ❑ Admission: $9.00 adult, $8.00 senior(60+), $5.00 child (3-17).

Permanent exhibits include galleries focusing on: Paleontology; Archaeology - detailing prehistoric Native American cultures; Kentucky, Naturally! focusing on local wildlife; 19th Century History featuring home life, politics, Underground Railroad & the Civil War; and River Heritage specializing in steamboats and tugs. All permanent exhibits include touchable objects to supplement learning. Additionally, special activities and exhibits include historic toys and trains available for play. Kids, look for the shrunken head!

CARNEGIE VISUAL & PERFORMING ARTS CENTER

1028 Scott Blvd.

Covington 41011

- ❑ Phone: (859) 491-2030. **www.kentuckycenter.org**

Four art galleries showcase regional artists. Free year-round arts education programs for youth (ArtStop). The theatre hosts a variety of performance events including Christmas and Appalachia productions and workshops on things like making drums.

MAINSTRASSE VILLAGE

616 Main Street (I-75 exit 192)

Covington 41011

- ❑ Phone: (859) 491-0458 or (800) STAY-NKY

www.mainstrasse.org

❑   Note: Northern Kentucky Visitors Center next to bell tower.

Goose Girl bronze sculpture 2 blocks east of tower.

Ongoing restoration and revitalization of a 30 block area in west Covington is now a village with shops and restaurants (try some sweets at the Strudel Shop near the Tower). A favorite with kids is the Carroll Chimes Bell Tower in Goebel Park. The 100 foot bell tower with a 43 bell carillon plays on the hour, from 9:00am-dusk, spring thru Christmas. The bell tower contains one of the 2 American-made animated clocks in the world, with 21 figures performing "The Pied Piper of Hamelin".

RAILWAY EXPOSITION MUSEUM

315 West Southern Avenue

Covington 41011

❑   Phone: (859) 491-7245

❑   Hours: Saturday-Sunday 12:30-4:30pm (May-October)

❑   Admission: $4.00 general

Interiors of railroad cars, railroad memorabilia and locomotives displayed are displayed at this educational museum. Guided tours of pullman sleepers, diner, business cars, training cars, caboose, engine cars, kitchen cars, postal cars, and troop carriers.

KINCAID LAKE STATE PARK

Rural Route 1, Box 33 (I-275 east to US 27 south to KY 159)

Falmouth 41040

❑   Phone: (859) 654-3531

http://parks.ky.gov/parks/recreationparks/kincaid-lake/

A great big campground with a giant lake makes this popular for fishermen, boaters and campers. Explore the unspoiled beauty and variety of nature habitats at Kincaid Lake State Park on two hiking trails. Named for the native flora, the Spicebush and Ironwood Trails offer 2.25 miles of connected loop trails. Great for watersports, hiking trails, pedal boats, outdoor pool, tennis and mini-golf too.

KENTUCKY WOOL FESTIVAL

Falmouth. Once a strong area sheep industry town, now the area maintains its heritage with demos on sheep shearing and sheep dog herding, wool spinning, sorghum and corn products, ethnic foods and a petting zoo. Admission. **www.kywoolfest.org** (first full weekend in October)

AUTUMNFEST

Georgetown. Bi-Water Farm (US 25N), 5 miles north of KY Horse Park. Farm festival full of color and fall food and hayrides. **www.biwaterfarm.com** Admission. (weekends mid-September thru October)

FESTIVAL OF THE HORSE

Georgetown. Downtown. Central Kentucky's premiere horse festival with a family orientation featuring entertainment, food, a children's parade and of course, a horse show. **www.festivalofthehorse.org** (end of September beginning of October weekend)

GREENBO LAKE STATE RESORT PARK

HC 60 Box 562 (I-64 Grayson exit on KY 1 north)

Greenup 41144

❑   Phone: (606) 473-7324

http://parks.ky.gov/parks/resortparks/greenbo-lake/

The name Jesse Stuart (author, educator, Kentucky Poet Laureate and a native of Greenup County) is found throughout these hills at both the lodge and state nature preserve. Read the poet's work in the reading room, swim in the lakeside pool with waterslide, children's wading pool and mist fountains or hike in secluded forests and trails (the Jenny Wiley Trail Heritage Byway). Enjoy a variety of entertainment each summer in the outdoor amphitheater, including "Battle of the Bands", high school drama productions, concerts, music festivals, arts and more. Pets are allowed if restrained. The lodge's restaurant features catfish dinners and local products. There's also a campground, marina and rental boats, pool, tennis and mini-golf.

ASHLAND, THE HENRY CLAY ESTATE

120 Sycamore Road (I-75 exit 104, turn left, go 7.5 miles. Corner of Sycamore and US 25/KY 922)

Lexington 40502

- ❑   Phone: (859) 266-8581. **http://www.henryclay.org**
- ❑   Hours: Tuesday-Saturday 10:00am-4:00pm, Sunday 1:00-
      4:00pm.Closed Mondays (November-March). Closed January,
      February and holidays.
- ❑   Admission: $10.00 adult, $5.00 child (6-18).
- ❑   Tours: one hour long - guided, given on the hour.
- ❑   Note: Food is available in the Ginkgo Tree Café on the brick
      patio outside, is open for lunch and snacks. Museum Store.
      Educators: click the Learn page for links to Artifact Adventure.

Henry Clay (1777-1852) was named The Great Compromiser, Harry of the West, candidate for President and quoted "I'd rather be right than president". For more than forty years, Henry Clay lived at Ashland, the place he loved best. When he was at home he could be seen frequently pacing the "Henry Clay Walk" that still runs through the trees behind the main house. Many of the great speeches which he delivered in Congress were composed along these peaceful walks.

Living here most of his adult life, the 18 room mansion is furnished with Clay family possessions. The tour begins with a videotape historical review. On tour, there are also outbuildings on the grounds like the icehouse, smokehouse, dairy cellar, and privy/laundry and keepers cottage - all in a park-like setting.

CIVIL WAR CHRISTMAS Ashland. Open house with holiday decorations, music and refreshments. Admission. (second weekend in December)

For updates visit our website: www.kidslovetravel.com

OLD KENTUCKY CANDIES

450 Southland Drive (I-75 exit 115 west to Harrodsburg Rd, right on Lane Allen Road to Southland)

Lexington 40503

- ❑ Phone: (859) 278-4444   **www.oldkycandy.com/**
- ❑ Admission: FREE
- ❑ Tours: Monday-Thursday 10:00am-12:30pm and 1:30-3:00pm. 45 minutes. Best to call ahead for production hours. 8 to 50 people for tours. Reservations please.

Hopefully you'll go on a day when you can watch them make Kentucky Derby Mints or UK molded chocolates. Plenty of samples follow the tour that includes verbal and photo explanations. If you don't reserve a tour ahead of time, you can still enjoy the viewing and especially the sampling!

MC CONNELL SPRINGS

416 Rebmann Lane
(New Circle to Old Frankfort Pike, exit 6 south, follow signs)

Lexington 40504

- ❑ Phone: (859) 225-4073   **http://www.mcconnellsprings.org**
- ❑ Hours: Daily 9:00am-5:00pm.
- ❑ Admission: generally FREE
- ❑ Educators: download interpretive notebooks here: **www.mcconnellsprings.org/education.html**. Note: each month they have at least two weekend special events - this is the best time to visit as interpreters are on hand to demo pioneer activity. Unless you're with a group tour during the week, the park's historical buildings aren't that interesting to just peek into the windows.

In June 1775, William McConnell and his fellow frontier explorers camped at a natural spring in the wilderness of the Virginia territory known as Kentucky. Word came from nearby Fort Boonesboro that the first battle of the American Revolution had been fought in Lexington, Massachusetts. In honor of the battle, the group named their future settlement "Lexington".

McConnell Springs is the site where Lexington was founded. It lies within a tract of land claimed by William McConnell in 1775. McConnell Springs has over two miles of trails that wander past historic foundations, stone fences, an old farm pond and lush vegetation. The new Education Center is equipped with a lab with sinks and counter space allowing students to conduct hands-on experiments and textbook research.

DID YOU KNOW? This is the campsite of the first settlers in the Bluegrass.

PARKETTE DRIVE-IN

1216 E. New Circle Road (I-75 exit 110 head west on US 60 to south on New Circle Road a couple miles on the right)

Lexington 40505

❑   Phone: (859) 254-8723 **http://theparkette.com/**
❑   Hours: Open at 11:00am Monday - Saturday.

Very economically priced (combo meals are under $4.00), this place is a step back in time. Since 1951, this "drive-in" ordering eatery is right out of scenes of "Happy Days". After placing your order over the microphone, a delivery girl or boy (adorned in Parkette cap and t-shirt or poodle skirt of the 50's) delivers you order window-side. Their menu includes burgers, fried chicken, seafood and the famous "Kentucky Poor Boy" sandwich (double-decker burgers dressed with toppings to the hilt!). Memories meet the pavement when (on Friday nights) the Parkette is host to classic cars and motorcycles. They serve 12,000 customers a week.

UNIVERSITY OF KENTUCKY

South Limestone Street (Visitor Ctr is at UK Student Center off Ave of Champions bounded by Limestone St, Euclid Ave., & Rose St)

Lexington 40506

❑   Phone: (859) 257-9000   **www.uky.edu (campus guide/map)**
❑   Admission: FREE
❑   Tours: Walking tours are conducted Monday-Friday at 10:00am

and 2:00pm (also Saturday at 11:00am during the academic year). Guided tours of the campus depart from the visitors center in the Student Center on Euclid Avenue across from Memorial Coliseum.

❑   Note: a good stop to catch some Wildcat Fever or just stretch your legs admiring exhibits, inside or outside. Admission is FREE!

The 625 acre campus was established in 1865 and enrolls 24,000 students.

UK ART MUSEUM - Singletary Center for the Arts at the corner of Euclid and Rose Streets. Changing shows of permanent and traveling exhibits. Tours available. Tuesday-Sunday, Noon-5:00pm. Closed July 4, Thanksgiving, and Christmas thru New Years. (859) 257-5716.

WEBB MUSEUM OF ANTHROPOLOGY - Lafferty Hall, center of campus. Traces history of humans in Kentucky. Other displays highlight the artistry, ingenuity and technology of present-day cultures from around the world. Monday-Friday 8:00am-4:30pm. Closed holidays. (859) 257-7112.

COLDSTREAM & MAINE CHANCE FARMS - Newtown Park. Used by UK for crop and livestock research. North of downtown near I-64/75.

ARBORETUM PARK - "A Walk Across Kentucky" showcases state vegetation grouped by region. Open dawn to dusk. Children's Garden - Alphabet plants and plantings in old tennis shoes. Master Gardener - demo Veggie Garden, Fish Pond, plants for Kentucky gardens. Be sure to get a colorful map and have fun playing the Arboretum Garden Game. (859) 257-9339.

LEXINGTON CHILDREN'S THEATRE

418 West Short Street (downtown)

Lexington 40507

❑   Phone: (859) 254-9565. **www.lctonstage.org**
❑   Admission: $13-$16.00 each or subscription discount Flex-Tix pricing.

Charlotte's Web, a Christmas Carol, and A Wind in the Willows are examples of the many folklore-based plays offered. Plays are rated for age appropriateness (ex. Age 4+ or Age 9+).

LEXINGTON LEGENDS BASEBALL

Applebee's Park, 1200 North Broadway,

Lexington 40507

❑   Phone: (859) 422-7867. **www.lexingtonlegends.com/**

They may be a Single A team, but Lexington has quickly embraced their new team in a major league way and the seats are packed for home games. The park has a family picnic area and kids play area. The season runs from April to September. Kansas City Royals affiliate. Tickets run avg $7.00. Kids eat Free, Kids Club and Firework nights, too.

LEXINGTON PHILHARMONIC

161 North Mill Street (ArtsPlace), **Lexington 40507**

❑   Phone: (859) 233-7896 or (859) 233-4226 tickets
      www.lexphil.org

The Family Series (one-hour musical and visual with activities), Discovery Concerts, and Pops Concerts (Patriotic Concert, Kentucky Christmas Chorus, two free concerts and Picnic with the Pops). The PB&J series is for your little ones' ears and tummies. Eating PB&J sandwiches, playing with the instruments, and hearing a great concert is all part of the fun. ($5-7.00)

EXPLORIUM OF LEXINGTON

440 West Main Street (Victorian Square, corner of W. Short and Algonquin Streets),

Lexington 40507

❑   Phone: (859) 258-3256 **www.explorium.com**
❑   Hours: Tuesday-Saturday 10:00am-5:00pm, Sunday 1:00-
      5:00pm. Closed Mondays except some holidays and breaks.
      Closed Easter, week after Labor Day, Thanksgiving and
      Christmas.
❑   Admission: $7.00 per person (age 1+). Free parking for up to 3
      hours in Victorian Square Garage.

❏   FREEBIES: While you're downtown, stop by Thoroughbred Park
      on Main Street where 7 life size bronze statues of horses racing
      are available to climb on for great photo ops!

Hands-on exhibits cover science, nature, history, civics and
ecology. Little ones can visit Wonder Woods (under age 3 - hear,
touch and see nesting areas). Everyone will love to make huge
bubbles in the Bubble Zone; go Home to world geography and
culture; "Walk on the Moon" and even sit in a crater!; make a
Quake; be a Turtle; Greet the Brainzilla (giant brain that talks to
you); Walk thru a Human Heart with many "chamber" rooms;
make Me and My Shadow; or brush some giant teeth. Extremely
well done exhibits include descriptions that are easy to follow and
teach to the children. Exhibits change each season, so there is
something new to explore. Look for occasional new Dino, horse or
bubble themed exhibits. Have fun!

DID YOU KNOW? Drop-in Activities take place most Sunday
afternoons.

HUNT-MORGAN HOUSE

201 North Mill Street (near 2nd Street, downtown)

Lexington 40508

❏   Phone: (859) 253-0362
      www.bluegrasstrust.org/hunt-morgan.html
❏   Admission: $10.00 adult, $4.00 student with ID.
❏   Tours: Guided tours Wednesday-Friday 1:00pm-4:00pm,
      Saturday 10:00am-3:00pm, Sunday 1:00-5:00pm (mid-March to
      mid-December). Closed Thanksgiving. Tours begin ¼ past the
      hour.

An 1800's Federal-style prominent family home of the Hunt-
Morgan families. John Wesley Hunt was the first millionaire of the
west (and built this home).   John Hunt Morgan was the
"Thunderbolt of the Confederacy" and Thomas Hunt Morgan was
the "father of modern genetics" and a Nobel Prize winner. The
architecture of a fan-light doorway and cantilevered staircase
mixed with original furnishings and Civil War memorabilia, make
this a piece of history based on its inhabitants.

MARY TODD LINCOLN HOUSE

578 West Main Street (just a block down from the Rupp Arena)

Lexington 40508

- ❑ Phone: (859) 233-9999. **www.mtlhouse.org**
- ❑ Hours: Monday-Saturday 10:00am-3:00pm (March 15-November). Closed holidays.
- ❑ Admission: $10.00 adult, $5.00 child (6-12)
- ❑ Tours: Last tour begins 45 minutes before closing. Guided, one hour from 10am to 3pm.
- ❑ FREEBIES: Printable Word Search, Math Word Problems online under: Educational.

The girlhood home of Abraham Lincoln's wife, Mary. The two story, beautiful brick 1803 Georgian-style house is furnished with period furniture from Mary's collection and personal articles of the Lincoln-Todd families. Kids like hearing stories about a famous adult's life as a child. Did you know that Mary had 15 brothers and sisters and that she had a formal education of 12 years (vs. her husband who really had very little)? Opposites attract.

KENTUCKY HORSE PARK

4089 Iron Works Parkway (I-75 exit 120)

Lexington 40511

❑   Phone: (859) 233-4303 or (800) 678-8813
     www.kyhorsepark.com

❑   Hours: Daily 9:00am-5:00pm (March 15-October). Closed on
     Mondays and Tuesdays (November-March 14). Closed
     Thanksgiving, Christmas, and New Years.

❑   Admission: $12.00-$16.00 adult, $6.00-$8.00 child (6-12).
     Additional special exhibit fees may be added on during peak
     season (late spring thru late summer). Children 5 and under free
     when accompanied by paying adult. The lowest pricing is offered
     for the Winter Season (less activities available). Tickets include
     the International Museum of the Horse, the American Saddlebred
     Museum, trolley tour and equine presentations throughout the
     day.

❑   Note: Clubhouse Restaurant, Campgrounds, Gift Shop,
     Horseback rides ($2

5+),
Pony rides ($5+), Nearly 60 horse shows are held here yearly.
Visits with Mares and Foals daily presentation in June/July.
Educators: wonderful curriculum on the history of the horse is
online under: Educational Opportunities/ ATQH Curriculum.

Do you have a real horse lover in the family? This is a horse-lover's dream park. It's Kentucky's tribute to one of its famous industries from tiny minis to large draft horses to retired racing stars. Begin with the Visitor Info Center Film - wide screen film "Thou Shalt Fly Without Wings" - depicting man's special relationship with horses both at work and play. Now, go next door to the International Museum of the Horse. Before long, take the horse-drawn trolley tour. Then catch a show at the Hall of Champions - home of retired "equine millionaires" (3x daily). They tell you funny stories about famous horses. Also be sure to catch a show at the Parade of Breeds - show of dozens of breeds of horses with their riders in native costume with music accompaniment (2x daily). Some are used for rugged terrain, pulling, cowboy riding, cavalry, or trailing. Fill the time between shows at the Big Barn (talk with trainers), Draft and Breeds and Carriage Barns, farrier's and harness maker's shops. The American Saddle Horse Museum - is a multi-image show and exhibit hall located on the premises near the parking lots. (800- 829-4438).

FESTIVAL OF THE BLUEGRASS Kentucky Horse Park. Www.festivalofthebluegrass.com. The oldest bluegrass festival around with national bands (traditional, contemporary, ole tyme string style), workshops and kids activities. Admission. (second weekend in June-Thursday-Sunday)

SOUTHERN LIGHTS Kentucky Horse Park. With the Horse Park setting, drive thru 2.5 miles of animated displays of lighted holiday cartoon characters, many equine-themed action scenes, Cinderella's carriage and dinosaurs. Santa, mini-trains, performers, snacks and hot beverages are available too. Nightly 5:30-10:00pm. Admission per carload. (Saturday before Thanksgiving - December)

WAVELAND STATE HISTORIC SITE

225 Waveland Museum Lane, 225 Higbee Mill Road (Off US 27, south of downtown)

Lexington 40514

❑ Phone: (859) 272-3611
   http://parks.ky.gov/parks/historicsites/waveland/
❑ Hours: Wednesday-Saturday 10:00am-5:00pm, Sunday 1:00-5:00pm (March-December).
❑ Admission: $7.00 adult, $6.00 senior, $4.00 student (age 6+).
❑ Tours: On the hour, last tour 4:00pm. Tours last approximately 1.5 hours.
❑ Note: Picnic grounds. Country Picnic and tours (meal and tour several days each week in June, small additional fee for food).

This beautiful 1847 Greek Revival home was built by Joseph Bryan, a grand-nephew of Daniel Boone. Waveland exemplifies plantation life in Kentucky in the 19th-century; from the acres of grain and hemp waving in the breeze (hence the Waveland name), to the raising and racing of blooded trotting horses. Tours focus on the everyday lives of the Bryan Family and the African-Americans who lived and worked there. Included are the icehouse, smokehouse and servants quarters.

CHRISTMAS CANDLELIGHT TOURS Waveland. Open house tours at night with holiday decorations, music and refreshments. Admission. (second weekend in December)

RAVEN RUN NATURE SANCTUARY

5888 Jacks Creek Road (off US 25/421 south)

Lexington 40515

❑ Phone: (859) 272-6105 **www.ravenrun.org**
❑ Hours: Daily 9:00am-5:00pm. Trails close 30 minutes before park closing. Closed Thanksgiving and Christmas.
❑ Admission: FREE

Follow trails lined with native flora and fauna, rock fences, a historic home, meadow, forest and creeks leading to views of the Kentucky River palisades. Over 10 miles of hiking trails provide access to streams, meadows and woodlands characteristic of the area. Numerous 19th century remnants of early settlers, as well as over 600 species of plants, allow visitors to become acquainted with and appreciate the natural world. Raven Run also accommodates over 200 species of birds throughout the year. The park is also known for the waterfalls and wildflowers. Stop at the nature center hands-on exhibits, too.

AVIATION MUSEUM OF KENTUCKY

4000 Versailles Road (2 miles west of New Circle Rd. on US 60 to Bluegrass Airport Road)

Lexington 40544

❑   Phone: (859) 231-1219. **www.aviationky.org**
❑   Hours: Tuesday-Saturday 10:00-5:00pm, Sunday 1:00-5:00pm (April-December). Closed Thanksgiving, Christmas and New Years.
❑   Admission: $5.00-$8.00 (age 6+).

Most interesting to kids is the cockpit you can sit in, the supersonic trainer, and the "Women in Aviation" display. The Aviation Museum of Kentucky has interactive, hands-on exhibits. There are also lots of uniforms, model airplanes, actual aircraft (helicopters, a Skyhawk II, and a Quadraplane). There is a lot of walking around, inside and out, in places like this so enjoy the exit from the vehicle and get some exercise.

KEENELAND TRACK KITCHEN

4201 Versailles Road (US 60 west)

Lexington 40592

❑   Phone: (859) 253-0541. **www.keeneland.com**
❑   Hours: "Breakfast with the Works" buffet served during morning workouts during seasonal race months (usually April and October) daily 6:00am-10:30am and again for lunch (times vary). Otherwise, open daily except major holidays at 6:00am.

May be Closed Monday, Tuesday and Easter.

❑   Admission: Reasonably priced buffet (~$8).

Meet and greet and eat with trainers and jockeys at breakfast during morning workouts. You don't have to be a horseman to enjoy the food at Keeneland's track kitchen--but you might end up sitting near a famous jockey, trainer or owner when you do. What's on the buffet? Pure Kentucky southern breakfast of meats, biscuits, eggs, potatoes, grits and assorted light fare. They offer Free children's activities, including having photos made in pint-sized jockey silks. To walk off your breakfast, try wondering the paddock in the morning when its serene (unless its race month - then it's a hub of activity). Race months, morning walks give fans one last look at the magnificent horses before they run the race of their lives.

TOYOTA MOTOR MANUFACTURING KENTUCKY

1001 Cherry Blossom Way (I-75 exit 126 east - US 62 E, follow signs to "Visitor's Entrance"), **Lexington (Georgetown)** 40324

❑   Phone: (502) 868-3027 or (800) TMM-4485
      http://toyotaky.com/tour.asp
❑   Hours: Visitor Center – 8:30am-3:30pm weekdays; to 6:00pm on
      Thursdays only.
❑   Admission: FREE

Public Tours: Monday-Friday, 9:30am, 11:30am, and 1:30pm; with
      additional 6:00pm tour on Thursday only. Closed major holidays
      and 3rd week of July. Reservations strongly encouraged.
      Children must be at least 1st graders and accompanied by an
      adult. School tours are available for grades 4-12.

Can you imagine a building so BIG that it could house over 156 football fields side by side! Wow! When you arrive and begin your tour of Toyota's state-of-the-art North American manufacturing facility, you and your kids will certainly appreciate that you won't have to walk for this tour. Begin your tour at the Visitor's Center where you get a great taste of what to expect through several interactive exhibits that teach you all about the Toyota JIT (Just in Time) manufacturing philosophy.

After viewing a short informational film, you'll board an electric tram (complete with headphones – no loud factory noises here!), to

take you on your journey. See steel coils weighing over 34,000 lbs. pressed into body panels and over 700 robots working in precision to create both sedans and mini-vans at this plant. In fact, this is the only manufacturing facility in the world where you will see both vans and cars on the same assembly line at the same time (how do they do that!). Kids will especially love the welding robots that send sparks flying to the factory ceiling (viewed from a safe distance). There are over 4000 welds in each vehicle made. Make sure you tell your kids to watch for the "flying assembly workers" who float in and out of vehicles on specially made chairs (on long booms).

RUTH HUNT CANDIES

550 North Maysville (I-64 exit 110)

Lexington (Mt. Sterling) 40353

- ❑ Phone: (859) 498-0676 **www.ruthhuntcandy.com**
- ❑ Store Hours: Monday-Saturday 9:00am-5:30pm, Sunday 1:00-5:30pm.
- ❑ Admission: FREE
- ❑ Tours: Monday-Thursday 10:30am-Noon and 1:00-2:30pm. Best to make appointment in the summer (less production). Reservations for group tours, please

"You are about to taste a little bit of Kentucky's confectionery history!" In the early 1920s, Ruth Hunt made and served homemade sweets to her bridge club. They were so loved that she decided to open a small candy store in her home, packaging products in coffee tins. On tour, you'll see hot cinnamon suckers being formed on a huge old marble slab, giant copper kettles (how old might they be?), and nuts roasting in the oven. Most of these confections are still made from Ruth's original recipes. Their most famous product is the Blue Monday Sweet Bar - the chocolate covered, pulled cream candy center, melt-in-your-mouth legend. Let their Blue Monday sweets cure your "Blue Monday". They are also noted as the official assorted candies of Churchill Downs. The treat at the end is to sample a few fresh sweets!

BLUEGRASS STATE GAMES

Lexington. www.bgsg.org Kentucky's premier amateur athletic competition for participants and spectators in 30 different sports. Events are held in several different venues, in several counties in Central Kentucky. (weekends in July)

YATESVILLE LAKE STATE PARK

PO Box 767 (US 23 to Louisa, then west on KY 3)

Louisa 41230

- ❑ Phone: (606) 673-1490 or (606) 686-2361 marina.
  http://parks.ky.gov/parks/recreationparks/yatesville-lake/default.aspx
- ❑ Note: Eagle Watch Weekend - houseboat tours on the Lake to the eagle's nesting site. Programs, games and refreshments included in admission.

Yatesville Lake State Park is a 2,300 acre mountain reservoir located in Eastern Kentucky. Full service campsites and marina with rentals are the highlights of this park. The lake and river make for good fishing and along these waters are great scenic overlooks and play areas. An ADA-compliant fishing getty and scenic fishing lagoon may be found at our marina area. The Yatesville Lake is highly regarded for its bluegill, crappie, and bass fishing. The campground has modern and primitive sites. The Mary Ingles Trail is 3.5 miles of hiking.

MAYSVILLE FLOODWALL MURALS

216 Bridge Street (downtown riverfront)

Maysville 41056

- ❑   Phone: (606) 564-9411
- ❑   Hours: 24 hours a day
- ❑   Admission: FREE

Historical portrayals of the Ohio River by artist Robert Dafford of scouts, nobility who floated down the river, and settlers.

NATIONAL UNDERGROUND RAILROAD MUSEUM

115 East Third Street

Maysville 41056

- ❑   Phone: 606-564-3200
  http://www.cityofmaysville.com/contact/national-underground-railroad-museum/
- ❑   Hours: Wednesday, Friday and Saturday 10:00am-3:00pm
- ❑   Admission: Donations

The museum symbolizes a local effort to preserve and display artifacts that tell the stories of life on the Underground Railroad. The Maysville area is surrounded by freedom stations - crossing the Ohio River north was a preeminent step in escaping bondage.

PUMPKINFEST

Maysville. R Farm, 7172 Strodes Run Road. **www.r-farm.com** Corn maze, petting zoo, pumpkin patch, dog show, entertainment, pig train rides, hayrides, live demos, food. Admission. (last weekend in September, first weekend in October)

KENTUCKY FOLK ART CENTER

102 West First Street (I-64 exit 137, follow signs)

Morehead 40351

- ❑   Phone: (606) 783-2204. **www.moreheadstate.edu/kfac/**
- ❑   Hours: Monday-Saturday 9:00am-5:00pm

❏   Admission: FREE
❏   Note: Museum Store with original artworks, Library and rotating
       upstairs Gallery.

Visit the only museum of Kentucky Folk Art, housed in a renovated early 1900 grocery warehouse. In the Auditorium, watch a seven minute video narrated by Rosemary Clooney introducing visitors to the "World of Wonder" housed within the Center. Look for recycled material sculpted into George Washington, Dolly Parton, Uncle Sam and Ronald McDonald. There was a birdhouse in an old shoe (that's art?). Our favorite was "Precious Memories" - a monkey made with junk - can you find the cow and chess piece? Whimsical to religious to political statements are made through this art. While many are amusing, in many instances, the art that you see was born out of hard times of common man.

MINOR CLARK STATE FISH HATCHERY

120 Fish Hatchery Road (SR 801south (Off I-64), below dam.
Farmers/Sharkey exit)

Morehead 40351

❏   Phone: (606) 784-6872
❏   Hours: Monday-Friday 7:00am-3:00pm. Closed holidays.
       Viewing of display pool and ponds anytime.
❏   Admission: FREE

This is among the largest warm water hatcheries in the country with 300 acres, 111 ponds, and a few racers (give fish a chance to exercise). The display pool is wonderful with large and small largemouth bass, walleye, 2 varieties of striped bass, and muskie to view up close. Their main objective is to produce fish for Kentucky waters to enhance opportunities to catch trophy fish.

MOREHEAD STATE UNIVERSITY

University Blvd.

Morehead 40351

❏   Phone: (606) 784-5221 or (800) 654-1944
       www.morehead-st.edu or www.msueagles.com

Established in 1887, the 500 acre campus enrolls 8300 students and has a history of focusing on Appalachian peoples. The Cora Wilson Stewart Moonlight School building was once used for nighttime reading and writing classes for Appalachian people and an Appalachian Collection is found on the 5th floor of the Camden-Carroll Library Tower. Nearby (KY 377) is the MSU Farm Complex & Arena.

CAVE RUN STORYTELLING FESTIVAL

Morehead. Twin Knobs Rec Area in Daniel Boone Natl Forest. Enjoy America's best loved storytellers in a beautiful mountain lakeside setting. Let these talented artists take you away to other times and places through the intrigue of storytelling. Stories will be told in large tents on the shore of Cave Run Lake. **www.caverunstoryfest.org** Admission. (last full wkd in September)

BLUE LICKS BATTLEFIELD STATE RESORT PARK

PO Box 66 (US 68 northeast of Lexington)

Mount Olivet 41064

❑   Phone: (659) 289-5507
    http://parks.ky.gov/parks/resortparks/blue_licks/default.aspx
❑   Hours: Museum: Wednesday through Sunday 9:00am-5:00pm
    Summers, weekends only April and May. $3.00-$4.00 fee
    applies.

In 1782, Blue Licks was the site of the last Revolutionary War battle in Kentucky. Visit the Pioneer Museum where you can learn more about the battle plus history of why prehistoric animals, Indians, pioneers and 19th century Southerners came for the salt licks and soothing waters (view a 10 minute video plus tons of relics). The Nature Preserve protects a rare plant - Short's Goldenrod - the only place it's found in the world growing along the rocky buffalo trace. On the scenic Buffalo Trace walk along the trampled remains of an ancient buffaol path. On campus, there's a modern lodge with dining room, cottages, campgrounds, pool, hiking trail, mini-golf and recreation programs.

The restaurant is known for southern-fried catfish and country ham which is produced in Kentucky.

BATTLE OF BLUE LICKS RE-ENACTMENT Blue Licks Battlefield SRP. **Http://battleofbluelicks.org** The very last battle of the Revolutionary War is acted out with some light-hearted fun plus realistic living history. Period music and food served up, too. Event Admission. (3rd weekend in August)

NEWPORT AQUARIUM

One Aquarium Way (Newport on the Levee, I-71south or I-275 east to I-471 south exit 5 (Rt. 8) to parking garage).

Newport 41011

- ❑   Phone: (888) 491-FINS. **http://www.newportaquarium.com**
- ❑   Hours: Daily 10:00am-6:00pm.
- ❑   Admission: $23.00 adult, $15.00 child (2-12).
- ❑   Note: Sharky's Café, Gift shop. No strollers past the entrance.

As you take the escalator down into the ocean, you'll read thru a brochure that invites you to explore one million gallons of water. They use clear, seamless acrylic walls and tunnels that truly make you want to reach out and touch the fish. Everywhere you go, remember to look up, look down and keep your ears open - it truly is a place you have to see with all your senses. 60 different exhibits take you places you'd probably never go! Rivers of the World (knifefish); The Bizarre and Beautiful (flashlight

fish); Pirate Theatre (a movie ship - Yo, Ho, Ho!); Shore Gallery (touch pool where visitors can feel & examine creatures like Mermaid's Purses or tickle a Horseshoe Crab); Kingdom of Penguins - 16 King Penguins from Japan are set in a winter setting theatre with video monitor close-ups. Occasionally baby penguins are hatched and grown in the nursery here! If your knowledge of frogs is limited, hop over to the Frog Bog - an exhibit space featuring 30 species of frogs and a new Frogger-type video game with an interactive pad that lets kids do the jumping. The absolute highlight is the Surrounded by Sharks exhibit - 85 feet underwater! The tunnels take you thru a shark home - as your child presses his nose against the acrylic tube - wait - for the first shriek when a shark is sighted and comes right at you! Don't worry, it's a total thrill that's completely safe.

RIDE THE DUCKS NEWPORT

One Aquarium Way (Newport on the Levee, I-75 exit 192, head east or I275 east to I471 north), **Newport** 41011

- ❑ Phone: (859) 815-1439 or **http://newportducks.com/**
- ❑ Admission: $19.00 adult, $14.00 child (2-12).
- ❑ Tours: Summer hours daily 10:00am-8:00pm. Fall/Spring hours generally daily Noon - 5:00pm (subject to weather and groups).

Quack-Tastic Fun! Ride The Ducks Newport is a 40-minute amphibious sightseeing experience. Travel on land and water in one amazing vehicle. Tour the streets and then SPLASH into the Ohio River. From the water, explore the historic waterfronts of Newport, Covington, and Cincinnati. See the World Peace Bell, Newport Aquarium, Historic Riverside Drive, Great American Ballpark, Paul Brown Stadium and much more. Your Captain will en-tour-tain you with stories of past and present. Learn about Newport and Ohio history, the Ohio River, its famous personalities and its impact on the state and our nation. Find out about Greater Cincinnati's role in film, song and sports too. Use the famous Wacky Quacker to become a part of the show as you roam the streets. Free with every ride, the Wacky Quacker will grab locals' attention and get the Duck rocking as you roll through the city streets. We always suggest Duck tours for kids to have fun with historical cities and never get bored because they're having too much fun quacking - they never realize they're learning.

WORLD PEACE BELL EXHIBIT

425 York Street, **Newport** 41011

❑   Phone: (859) 261-2526

The World Peace Bell is the world's largest free swinging bell. It weighs 66,000 lbs., is 12 feet in diameter and 12 feet high. Its clapper alone weighs an amazing 6,878 pounds. The yoke in which it swings weighs an additional 16,512 pounds. This magnificent bell rings with a powerful, awe-inspiring, deep resonant tone that is truly a majestic symbol of freedom and peace. Bell swings and rings each day at noon.

BB RIVERBOATS

101 Riverboat Row, Newport Levee Docks (I-75 exit 192),

Newport 41017

❑   Phone: (877) BB-is-fun **www.bbriverboats.com**
❑   Admission: $16-$22.00 just sightseeing. Add $6-$16.00 if meal served. Children nearly half price.
❑   Tours: 1 1/2 hour sightseeing cruises on the Ohio River. Several times daily (best to call for schedule). Reservations Required (May-October). Concessions on board.

Docked at the foot of Madison Street, see the modern sternwheelers or old-time steamboat. Also theme cruises like mini-vacation, holiday or historical. Many cruises offer additional lunch, brunch and dinner cruise options. Sightseeing only cruises offer history of the river plus points of interest on the riverfront. One of the best ones for kids is the Pirates of the Ohio Cruise on Friday afternoons full of fun and games for the family. Don a pirate hat, eye patch and treasure map and see if anyone will have to "walk the plank."

JIM BEAM NATURE PRESERVE

(US 27 to Hall Lane, near Camp Nelson, to Payne Lane)

Nicholasville 40356

❑   http://www.nature.org/ourinitiatives/regions/northamerica/u
     nitedstates/kentucky/placesweprotect/jim-beam-nature-
     preserve.xml

Dolomitic limestone forms high "palisade" cliffs along the river and its tributaries. Protecting a portion of the Palisades of the KY River, this is a feeding havitat for rare bat species. The Jim Beam Nature Preserve is open 365 days a year from sunrise to sunset. Visitors may enjoy low impact activities that include hiking, boating, fishing, photography and bird-watching. To protect the unique habitat of the preserve, you must stay on the trails at all times.

Brooklyn Bridge On US Scenic 68

The River Palisades helped to make the bridge "one of the Show places of the Nation" - a magnificent scenic and historic spot. The approach from the Jessamine County side of the river at one time was through the Daniel Boone Tunnel (the first highway tunnel in the state) which can still be seen at the crossing. This location provides a spectacular view with fall foliage displays and spring flowering red bud and dogwood. The fabulous Kentucky River Palisades are a feature of this drive.

CAMP NELSON HERITAGE PARK

6614 Danville Road (US 27 south of Lexington)

Nicholasville 40356

❑   Phone: (859) 881-5716   www.campnelson.org
❑   Hours: Tuesday-Saturday 10:00am-4:00pm. Interpretive trails
     open dawn to dusk.
❑   Admission: FREE
❑   Tours: White House Tours run 10am-4pm.

The origin of Camp Nelson is closely linked with President Lincoln's desire to free pro-Union sections of east Tennessee from Confederate control. The camp supplied Union efforts in east

Tennessee, central and eastern Kentucky and southwestern Virginia. The only remaining building of the 300 within the camp is the White House which was seized from the residents, the Oliver Perry family. This house served as the Officers' Quarters and is open to tour to depict both the life of the Perry's and military life. A visitor can walk along the interpretive trail and imagine what it would have been like to have been stationed at Camp Nelson.

HARRY MILLER LOCK COLLECTION & MUSEUM OF PHYSICAL SECURITY

1014 South Main Street (Lockmasters Inc. training center)

Nicholasville 40356

- ❏ Phone: (859) 887-9633 **www.lsieducation.com/museum/**
- ❏ Hours: Monday-Friday from 8:00am-5:00pm
- ❏ Admission: FREE
- ❏ Tours: generally self-guided

See the world's largest lock collection. The museum houses locks from the 13th century to today. A brochure details the history of the items showcased. Especially note the Time Locks - even if you know the combination, you can only unlock the safe at a preset time and day - not automatically once the combination is input. It's a great place to see and learn everything about security. Even some spy stuff!

CARTER CAVES STATE RESORT PARK

344 Caveland Drive (I-64 west to KY 182 north)

Olive Hill 41164

- ❏ Phone: (606) 286-4411 or (800) 325-0059
  http://parks.ky.gov/parks/resortparks/carter-caves/default.aspx
- ❏ Admission to Caves: $7.00-$10.00 adult, $4.00-$5.00 child (3-12).

Tour through more than 20 twisting caverns departing from the Welcome Center several times daily. Bat Cave is the protected home of the Social Bat/Indiana Bat. You can learn about the Bat Hibernaculas in the Center however the caves are closed to tours for endangerment.

Cascade Cave, with a 30 foot underground waterfall or X Cave with formed luminous stone fans, pipes and spirals are special spots here too. X cave is named that because its passages cross in the center of the cave to form the letter "X." See if you notice that. Oh, and look out for Headache Rock.

Canoeing down Tygart's Creek (June-August) can be fun or take a guided horseback trail ride. The 20 miles of hiking trails feature such attractions as Box Canyon, Wind Tunnel and Natural Bridge. Property next to this park is Tygart's State Forest with many other trails. Other amenities are a lodge, cottages, campgrounds, a marina with boat rentals, tennis and mini-golf.

GRAYSON LAKE STATE PARK

314 Grayson Lake Park Road (I-64 west to exit 172, KY 7 south)

Olive Hill 41164

❑   Phone: (606) 474-9727

http://parks.ky.gov/parks/recreationparks/grayson-lake/default.aspx

Once a favorite campground for Shawnee and Cherokee Indians, this land is full of sheer sandstone canyons and gentle slopes. A launching ramp provides boaters access to Grayson Lake. The 74.2-miles of shoreline range from gentle slopes to scenic canyons. Located 3 miles from the park, a marina has everything you need for a great day on the lake: rental fishing boats and pontoon boats, bait, grocery and rest rooms. Marina open year-round; fee for boat rentals. Camping is still the favorite here, plus a beach/swimming, a boat launch, and hiking trails past the odd "lizard head rock."

CREATION MUSEUM

2800 Bulittsburg Church Road (I-75 exit 185 (I-275 west) to exit 11 south)

Petersburg 41080

❑   Phone: (888) 582-4253 www.creationmuseum.org

❑   Hours: Monday-Friday 10:00am-6:00pm, Saturday 9:00am-6:00pm, Sunday Noon-6:00pm. Petting Zoo hours are slightly shorter. Closed most Christian holidays. Winter hours shorter.

❑   Admission: $29.95 adult, $23.95 senior (60+), $15.95 child (5-12). Military personnel FREE with paid adult admission. Price includes Special Effects Theater and Petting Zoo. Online specials each season.

❑   FREEBIES: the sister website, **www.answersingenesis.org/kids** has some fun puzzles, coloring and the parents page link if you want to download study guides. Note: the Planetarium simulation shows are outstanding and worth the extra admission if you can afford to add it in.

The site's 60,000 square feet of family fun logo is: "Prepare to Believe", and it's true! Some call it a Dinosaur Museum- it's true. Some call it a Bible Museum - it's true. "Much of the experience features displays that would be similar to what you would find in a natural history museum, so you will see exhibits on par with some of the fine science museums around the world," said director, Mark Looy. "Because we're taking our visitors on a walk through history from Genesis to Revelation, it is a biblical museum combining Scripture with the best of what science can present."

Begin in the senses-shattering (and maybe beliefs-shattering) Men in White Special Effects Theater. A satire, two hip angels expose common myths about God and Creation thru thunder, rain, wind and lightning effects that you actually feel!

Next, kids can take their own route through a Canyon into the Dino dig site.

The museum then uses a series of realistic dioramas to explore Biblical relevance - Old scholars and contemporaries. Walk through a Time Tunnel into the Six Days of Creation Theater for yet another opportunity to sit down and visually stimulate your mind. Now, walk thru a simulated Garden of Eden, past the Tree of Life. As sin then sets in, Corruption Valley begins. Help Noah and his family prepare at the giant Ark Construction Site. After the

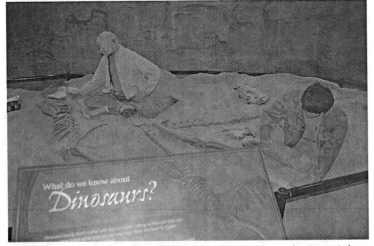

flood came Confusion at Babylon yet redemption at the Last Adam Theater (again, another great spot to sit down and take it all in). The final areas are all about kids - Dinosaur Den, the Dragon Theater (yes, dragons were real!) and an interactive Children's Play Area.

Finally, grab a snack or ice cream treat and walk the winding trails outside including two swinging bridges and a misty swamp area. The Petting Zoo is open, too. Guests are able to watch sheep and llama shearing, hoof trimming and get up close with all kinds of animals.

All will find answers to perplexing questions like: Why am I here? How old is the Earth? What really happened to the Dinosaurs? And, if you still don't know, purchase one of hundreds of related books for young and old in the Dragon Hall Bookstore. We all learned so much, so easily - I think our kids, the most. Well worth the admission price, friends.

BIG BONE LICK STATE PARK

3380 Beaver Road (I-75 AND KY 338, exit 175, follow signs)

Union 41091

- ❑ Phone: (859) 384-3522

   http://parks.ky.gov/parks/recreationparks/big-bone-lick/default.aspx

- ❑ Hours: Museum daily 8:00am-4:00pm (April-October). Monday-Friday 9am-3pm (November-March). Discovery Trail open daily dawn til dusk.

- ❑ Admission: FREE. Fee for campground and mini-golf.

- ❑ Note: Campground, Gift shop, Pool, 2.5 miles of Hiking Trails, Tennis, Mini Golf, Picnicking.

The birthplace of American Vertebrate Paleontology. A premier archeological site because great herds of giant mastodons, mammoths, and bison came to the warm salt springs (the springs still bubble today). Some became trapped in the marshy ground and died here, leaving skeletons that have been uncovered from prehistoric times. A walking diorama, the outdoor museum hosts these beasts displayed in their natural habitat. Erosion may still reveal bones (look for them on your hike) especially along the creek. Great buffalo herds once roamed this area and provided food, clothing and shelter for the Indians and  pioneers. Hunted to near extinction, the last wild buffalo was seen in Kentucky around 1800. A live buffalo herd now roams the property and your kids can touch Mastodon teeth!

BIG BONE LICK SALT FESTIVAL Big Bone Lick SP. A festival devoted to exploring the significance of area salt licks to early pioneers with demos and crafts. (first long weekend in October)

BLUEGRASS SCENIC RAILROAD AND MUSEUM

Woodford County Park (US 62 west)

Versailles 40383

❑ Phone: (859) 873-2476 or **www.bgrm.org**
❑ Hours: Museum & train rides open every weekend 12:30-4:00pm. (early May thru mid-November).
❑ Admission: $12.00 adult, $10.00 child (2-12). Museum free.
❑ Tours: Departures 1-2 times per afternoon. Several Train Robberies and Holiday train weekends too.

Ride on the old Louisville Southern Mainline past horse farms, Kentucky wildflowers, through the rolling Bluegrass Regions, past a 240-foot deep gorge and on to the rugged terrain of the Kentucky River bluffs. The excursions are 1.5 hours long and are narrated. The depot museum is dedicated to the construction, restoration and preservation of the railroad arts and artifacts. There are interactive displays including a working telegraph set that visitors can use to send Morse code messages. Their theme train rides are the best way for younger children to enjoy the long ride (esp. the Clown Days) unless you ride during naptime!

SANTA EXPRESS Bluegrass Scenic Railroad. Train rides with Santa and treats. Admission. (Thanksgiving-December weekends)

JOUETT HOUSE

255 Craig Creek Road (Off McGowan's Ferry Road west, KY 1064)

Versailles 40383

❑ Phone: (859) 873-7902. **www.jouetthouse.org**
❑ Hours: Monday 10am-Noon, Friday Noon-5pm, Saturday 10am-5pm, Sunday 1:00-5:00pm (April-October)
❑ Admission: FREE

Have you ever heard of the "Paul Revere of the South"? Well, by touring the 1798 home of Captain Jack Jouett, you'll learn how he reportedly rode horseback for 40 miles to Charlottesville, VA to warn delegates of the British Invasion. Jouett migrated to the

Bluegrass after the war, where he played an important role in the Kentucky statehood convention, served in the legislature, and became a prosperous planter and breeder of fine horses and cattle. The house contains three rooms with painted fireplace mantels, a stone-lined cellar, and two bedrooms accessed by a sharply turning stairway. Jouett's son, Matthew's famous paintings are also on display.

NOSTALGIA STATION TOY AND TRAIN MUSEUM

279 Depot Street (off US 60 bypass, corner of Depot & Douglas)

Versailles 40383

❑ Phone: (859) 873-2497 **www.bgrm.org/#/nostalgia-station/4514702157**
❑ Hours: Wednesday-Saturday 10:00am-5:00pm, Sunday 1:00-5:00pm; closed major holidays.
❑ Admission: $1.50-$3.50 (age 3+).

A model train museum housed in a restored 1911 railroad station with exhibits of a reproduction of a 1926 Lionel train display and many children's toys. Also on display are operating layouts including a re-creation of a 1930s Lionel store with famous pre-war pieces. The displays are meticulously authentic to the original time period.

HARRIET BEECHER STOWE SLAVERY TO FREEDOM MUSEUM

2124 Main Street

Washington 41096

❑ Phone: (606) 759-0505
❑ Hours: Saturday Noon-4:00pm. All other days guided tours offered at the Washington Visitors Center.
❑ Admission: Donations accepted.

This is where the author of "Uncle Tom's Cabin" first witnessed a slave auction (1833) described in the book. The facility shows facets of a slaves life including shackles and art.

SORGHUM FESTIVAL

West Liberty. Old Mill Park, Morgan Cty Fairgrounds. The mule-drawn cane mill, steaming vats, and little jugs of sorghum molasses set the stage for three full days of Kentucky mountain heritage. Live music, a parade, the Old Country Store, Sorghum Queen crowned at annual Bowl Game, and 100 art and craft displays fill West Liberty. (fourth weekend in September)

DANIEL BOONE NATIONAL FOREST

1700 Bypass Road (KY 801), **Winchester** 40391

❑   Phone: (859) 745-3100

    www.stateparks.com/daniel_boone.html

❑   Hours: 24 hours a day. Specific hours for facilities within the
    park are listed below.

❑   Admission: FREE

The U.S. Forest Service maintains almost 700,000 acres of timberland in portions of 21 counties in eastern Kentucky stretching from Morehead in the north to the Tennessee border in the southeast. 800 miles of paved road and 500 miles of trails make the natural beauty and recreational facilities accessible (campgrounds, picnic and shelter areas, beaches and boat ramps - most on KY 801). Some facilities featured:

GIANT CANADA GEESE OBSERVATION AREA - largest of 11 subspecies of Canada geese. Mature ganders may have a wind span of 6 feet. Observation deck and interpretive trail.

CAVE RUN LAKE - I-64 exit 133, south on KY 801. 8000+ acre lake with 13 ramps, two marinas, 3 campgrounds, boating, swimming, horseback riding, mountain biking and hiking trails and fishing. Cave Run Dam is on KY 826 off KY 801 and has recreation facilities. The Cave Run Lake Morehead Ranger Visitor Center is two miles south of US 60 and has exhibits and a video presentation about the lake area. (606) 784-5624 from 8:00am-

4:30pm (Memorial day thru October) and open weekdays only the rest of the year.

PIONEER WEAPONS HUNTING AREA - US 60, south on KY 211 at Salt Lick to Rd. 129.   Over 7000 acres full of hiking and primitive weapons (only!) hunting of deer, turkey, grouse, squirrel, fox and raccoon. (606) 784-6428.

SHELTOWEE TRACE NATIONAL RECREATION TRAIL - almost 300 miles of trails. Sheltowee means " Big Turtle" and was the Indian name given Daniel Boone by the Shawnee who adopted him as the son of Blackfish, the great Indian war chief.

RED RIVER GORGE - Mountain Pkwy. Exit 33 at Slade is 27,000 acres of spectacular boulder-strewn areas of woodland, streams and waterfalls, sandstone cliffs, overlooks, arches, the Nada old logging railroad tunnel, and rare plant and animal life.   The Visitor Info Station is the Gladie Historic Site (606) 663-2825, on KY 715, and has info on recreation in the Forest. Open daily 10:00am-6:00pm (April-October). The Gladie Historic Site is a restored log cabin (c. 1880) with displays of early logging and farm life and many seasonal events. Here you'll find more information on the 38 miles of 150 sandstone arches - Gray's Arch on KY 15E being a stop where you can picnic on the ridge.   Clifty Wilderness off KY 15W are vertical sandstone cliffs, numerous arches, rock houses (cliff overhangs used as shelter by primitive peoples), rippling streams, waterfalls, primitive camping, hiking and canoeing.   Rock Bridge off KY 15W is a stone arch spanning Swift Camp Creek and Sky Bridge is another stone arch at the top of the ridge with a vista of the Red River Gorge.

NATURAL ARCH SCENIC AREA - off US 27S. Sandstone arch that's 100 feet wide and 60 feet high. (606) 679-2010

NOTES
-

Chapter 3
Area - South Central (SC)

Our Favorites...

* Corvette Assembly Plant - Bowling Green

* Lost River Cave & Valley - Bowling Green

* Mammoth Cave Area, Amusement, Museums - Cave City

* Wigwam Village - Cave City

* McDowell House & Apothecary - Danville

* Kentucky Down Under - Horse Cave

* Big South Fork Area - Stearns

* Lake Cumberland Area

"Corvette Fun" - Bowling Green

A QUICK TOUR OF… SOUTH CENTRAL KENTUCKY

Lost River Cave and Valley in Bowling Green is full of wonderful stories of famous inhabitants. The only floating cave tour in Kentucky, the cave area dates back thousands of years. It has provided shelter for Native Americans, both Confederate and Union soldiers, and even the notorious Jesse James and his gang. You'll also see a bottomless "Blue Hole" and hear the mysterious stories surrounding those who fall in it. Your tour will board a long boat and venture into the cave with only a flashlight. It's a small test of nerves as you go deeper into the cave, but the guide is careful to keep the mood "light" and talkative.

Before you leave Bowling Green, a "must stop" is the Corvette Assembly Plant Tour. Your kids will be amazed as they watch a newly built sports car "come to life". Follow the new car as it's driven off the line into the indoor testing booth. Watch the car earn its reputation for speed and handling!

Many go to the far western side of the region for the nationally known, Mammoth Cave. We'd advise making reservations ahead of time, especially if you want to take the Historic Tour or a specialty tour. We recommend starting with the basic, short (~1 hour) tour for young families. Kids ages 10+ will want to explore more underground terrain…especially the Snowball Room picnic area. Be on the lookout for troglodytes – animals adapted exclusively to darkness. Evening programs around the campfire are tempting as is the Miss Green River II riverboat tours through winding limestone cliffs and secret cave entrances.

We must admit, there's more to Cave City than just Mammoth Cave. What about going "sleepy in a teepee"? At Wigwam Village, you can spend the night in wigwams (permanent teepees) equipped with heat, A/C, private bath, and TV. You can meet your wigwam neighbors at the gathering place in the middle of the complex complete with grills, a playground, and a misting deck to cool off.

Other favorites in the area are Jellystone Park Camp Resort and Joe's Diner 1950's style restaurant. The Mammoth Cave Wildlife Museum is full of over 1600 stuffed wildlife from around the world. The white, cave-like hallways wind to and fro. Look for reindeer, giant moose, lobster, porcupine and giant Polar Bear.

As you enter or leave the Mammoth Cave area, Kentucky Down Under is a wonderful interactive nature park that truly helps you experience Australian wildlife. Have you ever touched a kangaroo?; fed a baby lamb?; watched Border Collies herd sheep?; learned to toss a boomerang?; danced to the Aborigines Welcome Song?; played the didgeridoo?; tasted Aussie food?; or walked amongst wallabies and their joeys? Wow, what an unforgettable family day! Please don't forget your camera here.

Lake Cumberland is probably what defines summer best...pleasure boating, fine fishing, comfortable lodging and numerous nature centers. Many state parks are found near, or on, the lake, so don't be afraid to explore the area...by foot or boat.

Not too far from the Cumberland area is Stearns, Kentucky and the Big South Fork National River and Recreation Area. Although sparsely settled, you'll see remnants of area industry. The Blue Heron Coal Mining Camp has recorded voices of the people who actually lived and worked in the village. They tell their story from inside "shell structures" representing simple homes, a church, a school, a bathhouse and a company store. You can take a scenic ride to Blue Heron aboard open-sided rail cars that are pulled thru steep-walled canyons and alongside streams. Try a Coal Miners Special at the Whistle Stop Café.

You don't get many chances to see an old-time famous doctor's house and apothecary...but, in Danville, you get a fabulous glimpse into Dr. Ephraim McDowell's House. He is famous for performing the world's first successful abdominal surgery on Christmas Day, 1809, while the patient sang hymns. See the actual "operating bedroom" and look for the giant green jar near the window of the apothecary. Why do pharmacies always have a green jar on display?

The South Central Chapter at a Glance...

Bee Springs

- Nolin Lake St Pk

Bowling Green

- Beech Bend Park
- Chaneys Dairy Barn
- Lost River Cave
- Natl Corvette Museum & Factory
- Russell Sims Aquatic
- Western KY Univ
- Duncan Hines Fest
- Balloons, Tunes & BBQ
- Riverview @ Hobson Grove Christmas

Burkesville

- Dale Hollow Lake St Pk

Burnside

- General Burnside Island

Campbellsville

- Green River Lake St Pk

Cave City

- Big Mikes Mystery
- Dinosaur World
- Floyd Collins Mus
- KY Action Pk
- Jellystone Park

- Mammoth Cave Wildlife
- Wigwam Village
- Hidden River Cave
- KY Down Under
- Mammoth Cave
- Diamond Caverns

Danville

- McDowell House
- Pioneer Playhouse
- Great Amer. Brass Band Fest
- Constitution Sq Fest

Franklin

- Old Stone Jail

Jamestown

- Lake Cumberland

Lucas

- Barren River St Pk

Nancy

- Mill Springs Battlefield

Perryville

- Perryville Battlefield

Stanford

- William Whitley House

Stearns

- Big South Fork Rec Area & Scenic Railway

Thompkinsville

- Old Mulkey Meetinghouse

NOLIN LAKE STATE PARK

PO Box 340 (Follow the Western Kentucky Parkway to Leitchfield exit (107) onto KY 259 South. Then, access from KY 728 and KY 1827 north), **Bee Springs 42207**

❑   Phone: (270) 286-4240

   www.parks.ky.gov/parks/recreationparks/nolin-lake/default.aspx

The 5500+ acre lake is popular for boating and fishing with a marina and beach near the park. Facilities include boat rentals, cottages, camping and picnic areas. A 1.6 mile hiking trail is open year-round that has a small waterfall when the conditions are right. This trail is a moderate exercise so please ensure that you have proper hiking shoes and water.

A sand beach curves along the shore of the lake. There are no restrooms or bathhouse facilities.

BEECH BEND PARK

798 Beech Bend Road (31W south to Riverview Ave turns into Beech Bend Rd, I-65 exit 28)

Bowling Green 42101

❑   Phone: (270) 781-7634. **www.beechbend.com**
❑   Hours: Daily (Memorial Day-Labor Day) and weekends only (May, September) for Amusement Park. Car racing is offered March - November, usually Saturdays at 5pm. Central Time.
❑   Admission: $27.00-$30.00 per person (age 3+). The price includes free soft drinks, unlimited rides (excluding go-carts), Gold Rush Golf, Splash Lagoon Water Park (in season), daily live entertainment and Granny Jones' Petting Farm, free parking, free sunscreen, and free mats and tubes every day.
❑   Note: Year-round full service campground, party rooms.

This is actually a multi-purpose facility offering entertainment in car racing (stock and NHRA dragsters) and the improved amusement park featuring adult and kiddie rides. The smaller scale amusement park is easily family-friendly with rides like go-carts, bumper cars, merry-go-round, giant slide, Tilt-A-Whirl, Big Mac Truck ride, Western Train ride, Tornado, Fire House Fun Land,

Flying Dragon Roller Coaster, Deluxe Sizzler, Dizzy Dragon, Jitter Bug, mini-golf, a water slide, flume ride and swimming pool. The Kentucky Rambler has been ranked one of the top wooden roller coasters in the country every year. Splash Lagoon features a wave pool, lazy river and Tiki Island with seven water slides and a giant tipping bucket. Cyclone Saucers "fly" at high speeds. Wet, dry, fast or slow - you guys decide what kind of day you're in the mood for.

CHANEY'S DAIRY BARN

9191 Nashville Road

Bowling Green 42101

- ❏ Phone: (270) 843-5567. **www.chaneysdairybarn.com/**
- ❏ Hours: Monday - Saturday 6:00am-6:00pm, Sunday Noon-6:00pm. Open later on weekend nights.
- ❏ Tours: $7.00 per person, by reservation, twice daily (except Sunday) include a wagon ride, live milking demo, visiting baby calves, hands-on learning center, the Inflatable Jumping Pillow, and a scoop of ice cream. Families can participate in tours on Weekender summer tours or the Fall Corn Maze. (April-October)

Along with their ice cream that is made on the premises, they offer homemade sandwiches, soups, etc. Tours are offered many days, by reservation, and include a wagon ride to the dairy farm next door.

LOST RIVER CAVE AND VALLEY

2818 Nashville Road. Corner of Nashville Road, (31W) & Cave Mill Road (I-65 take Exit 20 onto William Natcher Parkway, travel 4 miles to Exit #4 (31W)

Bowling Green 42101

- ❏ Phone: (270) 393-0077 or (866) 274-CAVE **www.lostrivercave.com**
- ❏ Hours: Daily 10:00am-5:00pm (extended hours each summer). except Thanksgiving, Christmas and New Year's. Group tours available by reservation (call for details). Boat tours during winter months and inclement weather are subject to cancellation.

Central Time.

Admission: $16.95 adult, $11.95 child (4-11), $3.95 preschooler. Online coupon.

Tours: Tours leave at the top of each hour beginning at 10:00am and ending at 4:00pm.

The only floating cave tour in Kentucky, it's also "re-found" and run by some very enthusiastic, fun folks. Right under the street is a cave with a river that "Ripley's Believe It or Not" has claimed is the shortest, and deepest river in the world. You'll begin with the walking, history and nature portion of the tour. Recent additions to the property make this a 2 to 4 hour excursion. Check out the Butterfly Habitat enclosure on the trails. They also now have gem mining, a wild bird sanctuary and a wonderful, easy access, treetop bridge that takes you 20 steps from the tour path (eliminates those dreaded stairs back up!)

The cave and valley dates back 1000s of years ago when it provided shelter at one time or another for Native Americans, both Confederate and Union soldiers and the notorious Jesse James and his gang after they had robbed the bank in nearby Russellville. You'll also see a "Blue Hole" freak of nature for yourself and hear the mysterious stories surrounding those who fall in it. As you come to the cave's entrance, everyone will want to explore the giant dance floor in the popular underground big band nightclub from the 30's and 40's. Now, your group will board a long boat and the guide will use only their hand-held light to venture into the cave. It's a small test of nerves as you go deeper into the cave, but the guide is careful to keep the mood "light" and talkative. An adventure not to be missed by your family!

NATIONAL CORVETTE MUSEUM

350 Corvette Drive (I-65, exit 28)

Bowling Green 42101

- ❑   Phone: (800) 53-VETTE. **www.corvettemuseum.com**
- ❑   Hours: Daily 8:00am-5:00pm. Closed Easter, New Years, Thanksgiving and Christmastime. Central Time.
- ❑   Admission: $10.00 adult, $8.00 senior (55+), $5.00 child (6-16), $20.00 family.
- ❑   FREEBIES: KidZone Activities for Download: **www.corvettemuseum.com/kids/** Note: Family Events include holiday and summer events. Educators: Fun Resources - **www.corvettemuseum.org/teacher/teacher-resources**

What a great way to further enhance your visit to the Corvette Factory! Especially designed for Corvette enthusiasts, you will be treated to thousands of Corvette-related exhibits and more than 50 models of every vintage, including the coveted 1953 Corvette (one of only 300 produced). You will especially love the concept cars (cars that were tested in design, but not ever produced for sale). The Chevrolet Theatre sets the stage with a high energy film about special car. Experience the romance that has lasted over 50 years in the Nostalgia Area. Full-scale exhibits include: The Barbershop, A 1960's Service Station, 1960's Dealer Showroom, and "Route 66" which explores the feeling of spending a day with your Corvette on the open road. The Performance Area highlights the racing success of Team Corvette. Kids will love the Design and Concept Area that teaches how cars are first designed in clay through final  production. Be sure to bring your camera for some great "car and driver" shots. Note: A great virtual tour is on the website.

RUSSELL SIMS AQUATIC CENTER

2303 Tomblinson Way (at Preston S. Miller Park off of Veterans
Memorial Blvd.)

Bowling Green 42101

❑   Phone: (270) 393-3271
   www.bgky.org/bgpr/aquatics/index.php
❑   Hours: Daily 10:30am-6:30pm. Sunday open at Noon. CT
❑   Admission: $8.00 adult, $5.00 senior and youth (6-15), $4.00
   child (3-5). Twilight Fee (after 4pm) 1/2 price.
❑   Note: No outside food or drink allowed in the pool facility.
   Toddlers must wear swim diapers.

This community facility features a stainless steel 50-meter
swimming pool, a zero-depth entry area with interactive water play
structures like palm trees, tumble buckets and tea cups. Kids will
love the splash playground full of water squirting toys such as a
teeter totter, water cannons, spiral spray, water trikes and spray
balls. The center also features a butterfly slide, spiral water tunnel,
two double water slides and a concession area. Splash In!

WESTERN KENTUCKY UNIVERSITY

1400 Kentucky Street. Planetarium on State Street. (I-65 exit 28.
Follow 31-W to Western Kentucky University)

Bowling Green 42101

❑   Phone: (270) 745-2592. **www.wku.edu/kentuckymuseum**
❑   Hours: Monday-Saturday 9:00am-4:00pm, Sunday 1:00-4:00pm.
   These are times for museum only. Central time.
❑   Admission: $5.00-$10.00 general (age 6+). 1/2 price on Sundays.
   These are fees for museum only. All facilities are closed during
   holidays and school breaks.
❑   Educators: Worksheets abound:
   www.bgkymuseum.org/Teachers/PDFWorksheets

Within the walls of the KENTUCKY MUSEUM are the Felts Log
House; Main Street: Mirror of Change; Growing up Victorian: A
Kentucky Childhood; and, First American Roads, Rails and Rivers:
Warren County Then and Now. You might really like the space on
Duncan Hines (the packaged food and dessert company). There's a

wide assortment of prehistoric objects, pioneer relics, old-fashioned toys and musical instruments. Hardin Planetarium has a 40-foot dome housing a star projector, special effects projectors with show times on Tuesdays and Thursdays at 7:30pm and Sundays at 2:30pm. Call (270) 745-4044 for exact show times and info. Listen for the Cherry Hall Carillon chimes in the symbolic dome on campus.

CORVETTE ASSEMBLY PLANT

Louisville Road & Corvette Drive (I-65 exit 28)

Bowling Green 42104

- ❑   Phone: (270) 745-8419
     www.bowlinggreenassemblyplant.com
- ❑   Admission: $7.00 per person.
- ❑   Tours: Guided, Monday-Friday @8:30am, 11:30am, and 2:00pm.
     Tours are one hour and 15 minutes long. No cameras or
     purses/pouches allowed. Closed holidays, month of December
     and the 1st two weeks in July. Required age 7+. Closed-toe shoes
     required. Central Time.

Since 1953, people have been drawn to the mystic powers that only comes from America's true sports car...the Corvette. This 2 seat legend has been produced here for worldwide distribution since 1982. We were absolutely amazed at the careful planning and "close-up" experiences that you'll get from this walking (1-mile) factory tour. Begin your tour with an introductory film and then see photos from famous owners from all over the world in the gallery. You'll also have a chance to win Corvette souvenirs in a trivia contest while you're waiting for your tour to begin. (Hint: The only year a Corvette was not produced was 1983). Once on your tour, your heads will be spinning in all directions seeing body panels being assembled and welding robots in action. Then see "the body marriage" where the newly created body meets the frame, suspension components, and its "heart"... the powerful V-8 engine. Maybe Mom or Dad will even get to start and drive a newly produced car off the line! The final highlight is watching the newly produced cars (18 per hour) enter a special glass enclosed booth   for   acceleration   and   braking   tests.

Hear the car's engine growl to life and quickly accelerate to nearly 100 miles per hour and then come to a screeching halt. The car's tires spin specially made wheels in the floor which are connected to computers that measure all of the performance specifications. Aaah…if Corvette would only make a mini-van!

DUNCAN HINES FESTIVAL

Bowling Green. www.duncanhinesfestival.com The native son of the famous baking products is honored with activities, food (especially desserts) and music. Uncle Duncan's Duck Race. (second or third weekend in July)

BALLOONS, TUNES & BBQ

Bowling Green/Warren Cty Regional Airport. Hot air balloonists from all over the country will converge on Bowling Green to compete for more than $10,000 in prize money. Hot air balloon competitive events throughout the weekend, testing the skill set of some of the sport's best pilots. Hot air balloons on display Friday evening at dusk for the ever popular Balloon Glow – and tether rides, weather and wind permitting – with competitive events kicking off Saturday morning, including crowd favorite Hare and Hound competitive lift off Saturday afternoon, and the final fly-in event on Sunday morning. Also carnival, bouncy rides, bbq and nightly entertainment. FREE. **Http://balloonstunesbbq.com** (weekend after Labor Day in September)

RIVERVIEW AT HOBSON GROVE CHRISTMAS OPEN HOUSE

Bowling Green. 1100 West Main Avenue. Riverview, classic example of Italianate architecture--arched windows, deep eaves with ornamental brackets, & cupola. Painted ceilings. Began late 1850s, Confederate munitions magazine in winter 1861-62, & completed 1872. Tours & special events. A great family time to visit many elaborate homes that may be too stuffy or boring to tour (for kids) any other time of year. Open houses generally have extensive holiday decorations, music and refreshments served. Admission is charged. **Www.bgky.org/riverview** (270) 843-5565. Southern Kentucky Victorian style tours. (middle of December - week before Christmas)

DALE HOLLOW LAKE STATE RESORT PARK

6371 State Park Road (I-65 exit 43 or 53. KY 90 east, then south on KY 449 & KY 1206),

Burkesville 42717

❑ Phone: (270) 433-7431 or (800) 325-2282
http://parks.ky.gov/parks/resortparks/dale-hollow/default.aspx

❑ Admission: FREE

❑ Note: Eagle Watch Weekends (last two of January). Join other eagle watchers on open barge tours to view the bald eagle in its natural wintering habitat. Admission for programs & tours.

On a bluff overlooking a 28,000 acre lake, the modern lodge offers extreme comfort in a wilderness setting at Kentucky's southern border. There's great fishing, boating, swimming, hiking trails (most follow old logging roads along narrow ridge tops which form peninsulas into the lake), horseback riding and mountain biking. There's also a campground, marina and a pool at the lodge. The cliff top lodge, built of limestone and massive timbers, sits high on a bluff overlooking the 28,000-acre lake and surrounding woodlands. The 60 guest rooms feature private balconies and patios. Rooms are available by late afternoon, check out by noon, Central Time. Pets are not allowed. The campground also has six camping cabins they rent. Island View Restaurant - Enjoy a variety of menu selections from traditional Kentucky cuisine. Try Kentucky Favorites such as the Hot Brown, Fried Catfish or Country Ham. To add to the atmosphere, the restaurant has three walls of glass that allows you to sit back and embrace the breathtaking view of Dale Hollow Lake and its astonishing islands.

GENERAL BURNSIDE ISLAND STATE PARK

PO Box 488 (US 27, 8 miles south of Somerset)

Burnside 42517

❑ Phone: (606) 561-4104 or (606) 561-4192
http://parks.ky.gov/parks/recreationparks/general-burnside/default.aspx

During the Civil War, Union General Ambrose Burnside and his troops patrolled this island to keep watch for Confederate soldiers. General Burnside has gone down in history for his beard and moustache worn with clean-shaven chin - called a "burnsider"; now called a "sideburn". The Island Park is surrounded by Lake Cumberland. Most like the park for camping, fishing and boating. There's also a pool and recreation programs.

CHRISTMAS ISLAND

One million lights on this 3.5 mile tour through a wonderland of 200 lighted displays. Horse-drawn carriage rides. (weekend before Thanksgiving - day before New Year's Eve)

GREEN RIVER LAKE STATE PARK

179 Park Office Road (KY 55)

Campbellsville 42718

❑   Phone: (270) 465-8255

http://parks.ky.gov/parks/recreationparks/green-river/default.aspx

This land is where Confederate General John Hunt Morgan was captured after the Battle of Tebbs Band in 1863. The Atkinson Griffin House was the hospital set up for the defeated Confederates and now houses a battle diorama, weaponry, slide show and exhibits (Visitor's Center). Other amenities are the shoreline campground, beach, mini-golf, 20 miles of hiking trails and mountain biking. There's also a marina with rental boats.

BIG MIKE'S MYSTERY HOUSE

566 Old Mammoth Cave Rd (I-65 exit 53, Hwy. 70 W, straight on Hwy 235 @ Big Mike's Rock & Gift Shop)

Cave City 42127

❑   Phone: (270) 773-5144
❑   Hours: Open daily (except winter) at 9:00am. Closing times are seasonal. Central Time.
❑   Small Admission charged.
❑   Note: Kentucky's largest rock shop with gifts and toys.

For updates visit our website: www.kidslovetravel.com

Feel the force of gravity in a strange and mysterious way. See the old dinosaur skull.

DINOSAUR WORLD

711 Mammothcave Road (I-65 exit 53)

Cave City 42127

- ❑ Phone: (270) 773-4345. **www.dinosaurworld.com**
- ❑ Hours: Daily 8:30am-sunset (March-October). Other seasons, weather pending (call for seasonal closing times).
- ❑ Admission:$10.00-$13.00 (age 3+). Friendly pets on leaches are FREE.
- ❑ Note: Picnic areas, playground and gift shop. Dino Gem Excavation.

Take an outdoor step back in time viewing over 100 life-size dinosaurs. Want some questions answered about the dinos (like, are all these figures really dinosaurs, or something else)? They really try to educate here, too. There's a short educational film on dinos in a unique Movie Cave setting.

FLOYD COLLINS MUSEUM

1240 Old Mammoth Cave Road (KY 70, Wayfarer Bed & Breakfast)

Cave City 42127

- ❑ Phone: (270) 773-3366
- ❑ Hours: Daytime, Central Time.

Near the entrance to Mammoth Cave park, it was originally an early 1930's souvenir shop. While exploring Sand Cave in 1925, Floyd Collins caught his leg. They attempted rescue, but couldn't. His death was the most widely reported news events of that time. The museum is housed in a bed & breakfast.

KENTUCKY ACTION PARK AND JESSE JAMES RIDING STABLES

3057 Mammoth Cave Road (I-65 exit 53 to Hwy. 70 west)

Cave City 42127

- ❑   Phone: (270) 773-2560 **www.kentuckyactionpark.com**
- ❑   Admission: Based on activity. ~$5 for golf/go carts/bumper boats/etc. Guided tours (horse/zip) are $20-$45/person. All day and family passes available.

Play the western themed mini-golf course or ride the favorite alpine slide for a thrilling quarter of a mile. Then, watch on-site glass-blowing as you lick your ice cream cone or roast a hot dog or marshmallow at the fire pit. After your snack, ride the bumper boats, twin zip line (longest zipline in ky) or exciting go cart rides. Many who visit comment that their horse riding trails are fun and well lead by guides - good for that early horseback riding experience.

JELLYSTONE PARK@ MAMMOTH CAVE CAMP RESORT

1002 Mammoth Cave Rd (exit 53 off I-65. 3 miles from the Mammoth Cave entrance), **Cave City 42127**

- ❑   Phone: (270) 773-3840 or (800) 523-1854
  www.jellystonemammothcave.com
- ❑   Season: Mid-April - October. Rental Fees for accommodations are $50-$100 per night with $30 fee for campsites. Most planned activities are free with stay. Large slide, jumping pillow, mini-golf and some other more supervised play areas require a small fee.
- ❑   Note: Camp store, laundry, ice, propane, RV supplies, fast food snack shop and gift shop.

The offerings at the largest resort park in Kentucky include: Daily visits by Yogi, Boo-Boo and Cindy; a large swimming pool with toddler pool; 350' waterslide; Yogi's petting zoo; arts and crafts; outdoor movies/bonfires; music synthesizer, mini-golf; game room; bank shot basketball; beach volleyball; small rides; batting cages; athletic fields; hiking trails; hayrides.

For updates visit our website: www.kidslovetravel.com

MAMMOTH CAVE WILDLIFE MUSEUM

SR 90, 409 E Happy Valley St. (I-65 exit 53, east on SRKY 90)

Cave City 42127

- ❏ Phone: (270) 773-2255 **http://mammothcavewildlife.com/**
- ❏ Hours: Daily 9:00am-8:00pm (March-October). Weekends only (November-February). Central Time.
- ❏ Admission: $5.00 plus per person.

Here they have a collection of wildlife specimens from around the world - all mounted in scenes that resemble their natural surroundings. The white, cave-like hallways wind to and fro. Each of the 1600 stuffed wildlife are clean, beautiful and crisp. Look for our favorites: the reindeer, giant moose, lobster, porcupine, Kodiak bear and giant Polar Bear. This is the nicest, freshest wildlife museum we've visited in our multi-state travel.

WIGWAM VILLAGE

601 North Dixie Hwy. (I-65 exit 53 to SRKY90 to US 31W north)

Cave City 42127

- ❏ Phone: (270) 773-3381 **www.wigwamvillage.com**
- ❏ Hours: Year-round. Central Time Zone.
- ❏ Rates: Reasonable, most around $60.00 per night. Close to Mammoth Cave and Kentucky Down Under.
- ❏ Note: Heat and A/C, private bath, tile floor, no pets, TV w/ cable, gift shop, in-room coffee. Families should request rooms with two beds or rent two teepees (or plan to camp out on the floor of the bedroom). Grills and picnic shelter outside.

 "Sleep in a Wigwam!". 15 actual wigwams (a name for permanent teepees) for overnight stay. The dream of a man in the mid-1930's, they have become national treasures. This location is one of only two left open in the United States. Check in at the 52 foot tall center teepee and gift shop. The gift shop has cute ceramic teepees that

look just like your room for the night (be sure to purchase one as a souvenir of your stay - get one with your room number painted on it). The rooms are quaintly small and furnished with original 1930's hickory and cane furniture. Without the distraction of a telephone, you can meet your wigwam neighbors at the gathering place in the middle with a playground and Misting Deck to cool off on hot summer days. Definitely a great place to tell the folks at home about!

HIDDEN RIVER CAVE AND THE AMERICAN CAVE MUSEUM

119 East Main Street (I-65 exit 58, Rte. 218 east)

Cave City (Horse Cave) 42749

- ❑ Phone: (270) 786-1466. **www.hiddenrivercave.com**
- ❑ Hours: Daily 9:00am-5:00pm. Open 'til 7:00pm during the summer. Central time.
- ❑ Admission: $15.00 adult, $10 youth 62-15) for museum and cave. $6.00 museum only.
- ❑ Tours: Guided cave tours leave each hour from the museum. Tours may depart more frequently during the summer season.

"Visit the Incredible" and descend over 100 feet below the surface of the earth. Along with rushing underground water and odd-shaped structures common with caves in the area, there's also underground ruins of an 1890's era hydroelectric system. Hear the stories of how the cave was saved from pollution to become a model for conservation. The American Cave Museum is a showcase of exhibits about prehistoric cave explorers, modern cave spelunkers, cave lighting, and the story of the "Kentucky Cave Wars" (some of the funny things owners would do to attract tourists and some of the sad things that happened for the sake of exploration). Learn about groundwater science and conservation, mining and finally, a wonderful gallery of American Caves. The cave may look like others in the region but the museum is professionally done and covers all American caves - a nice add-on feature of this visit.

KENTUCKY DOWN UNDER / KENTUCKY CAVERNS

SR 235, 3700 L and N Turnpike Rd (I-65 exit 58 to KY 235 east)

Cave City (Horse Cave) 42749

- ❑ Phone: (270) 786-2634. **www.kdu.com**
- ❑ Hours: Daily 9:00am-4:00pm Extended hours spring/summer. Closed Thanksgiving, New Year's Day and Christmas. Central Time.
- ❑ Admission: Regular season (mid-March - October) $25.95 adult, $19.95 senior (62+) & students, $15.95 child (4-13).
- ❑ Note: Gift shops. Outback Café. Gem Mining. Most walkways are paved.

This wonderful interactive nature park helps you experience Australian wildlife. Have you ever touched a kangaroo? (Walkabout); fed a baby lamb by bottle or watched Border Collies

herd sheep - you'll hear "Away" & "That'll Do" just like in "Babe" (Woolshed); learned to toss a boomerang or danced to the Aborigines Welcome song or learned circular breathing to play the rhythms of the didgeridoo? (Corroboree); journeyed thru an ancient underground passage? (Mammoth Onyx Cave - 30 minute tours); looked at "frogmouth birds" up close?; tasted a bison burger and other "Aussie" favorites? (Outback Café open weekends or daily in the summer); walked among emus and wallabies with Joeys? (Walkabout); or walked in an aviary where exotic birds feed as they land on your arm, shoulder or head? (Land of Lories). Wow, what an unforgettable family day! Please don't forget your cameras here.

MAMMOTH CAVE NATIONAL PARK
(I-65 exit 53 OR I-65 exit 48, follow signs)
Cave City (Mammoth Cave) 42259

- ❑ Phone: (270) 758-2328 or (800) 967-2283
  www.nps.gov/maca
- ❑ Hours: Visitor Center 7:30am-7:00pm (Summers). 8:00am-
  6:00pm (Fall/Spring). 8:30am-4:30pm (Winter). Closed on
  Christmas. Central Time.
- ❑ Tour Admission: $13 adult, $4.00 senior, $8 youth. Held several
  times daily.
- ❑ Note: Surface Programs - like Sand Cave Almanac with cave
  exploring, trip to Floyd Collins family homeplace - walk in the
  footsteps of tragedy. Evening Programs - 8:15pm - like Myth &
  Mysteries of the Underworld - discussion of ancient and modern
  cave myths. Miss Green River II - one hour riverboat tour - wind
  between high limestone cliffs and pass cave entrances. 4-6
  cruises daily, April-October. (270) 758-2243. Moderate
  admission charged for cruises. Tickets at Visitor Center. Also
  fishing, boating, trails, lodging, cottages, camping and horseback
  riding.
- ❑ Educators: links to grade appropriate workbooks:
  www.nps.gov/maca/forteachers/curriculummaterials.htm

Native Americans discovered Mammoth Cave about 4000 years
ago and late 1700 settlers rediscovered the cave. By the War of
1812, slaves mined saltpeter from caves to be used to make
gunpowder. The park was officially established in 1941. There are
two worlds to explore - the underground and the surface world of
tall-treed forests, rivers and wildlife (you'll probably see a wild
turkey or deer cross your path on the way in). Mammoth Cave is
claimed to be the longest cave system discovered on earth - over
350 miles charted on 5 levels! On tour, it's promised you'll learn
something new. Did you know the science behind cave
formations? Carbonic acid is what forms the rock (the same
ingredient as in colas you drink!). Be on the lookout for
troglodytes - animals adapted exclusively to darkness. Some tours
lead to the Snowball Room where there's an underground picnic

area. Advance tour tickets may be purchased by phone or web and then picked up at the Visitors Center at least 30 minutes before tour departure. There are gobs of people there and on a summer weekday practically every popular tour is sold out. Please make advance reservations. Plan to spend one-half to a full day here. Concessions and dining are available. The most popular tours are listed below:

- ❑ <u>THE HISTORIC TOUR</u> - (2 miles, 2 hours). Emphasis on: Large trunk passages; oldest tour routes; cultural history. Best for school-aged kids who can walk for almost 2 hours.
- ❑ <u>THE FROZEN NIAGARA TOUR</u> - (1/4 mile, 1 1/4 hours). Emphasis on: Deep pits; high domes; dry cave passages; dripstone area at exit; dynamic cave being carved by water; animal life. Best for young ones - probably too short and boring for older kids.
- ❑ <u>MAMMOTH CAVE DISCOVERY</u> – (1/2 hour, ¾ mile). Visit the Rotunda, one of the largest rooms in the cave, explore a vast canyon passageway, and learn about 19th-century saltpeter mining operations and the geologic origins of Mammoth Cave on this self-guiding tour. Includes part of the Historic and the full Mammoth Passage Tour routes.

DIAMOND CAVERNS

Rt. 255, 1900 Mammoth Cave Pkwy (I-65 exit 48)

Cave City (Park City) 42160

- ❑ Phone: (270) 749-2233. **www.diamondcaverns.com**
- ❑ Hours: Open year-round. Central Time. Closed only Christmas & Thanksgiving Days. 9:00am-5:00pm (until 6:00pm Summer, slightly shorter hours in fall/winter).
- ❑ Admission: $16 adult, $8 child (4-12).
- ❑ Tours: ½ mile long, guided. Tours leave every 30 minutes, daily.
- ❑ Note: Gift shop, dining in the Brass Lantern Restaurant Café.

This cave has been open since 1859 and is known for its state-of-the-art lighting of the live calcite formations. As in many caverns, there's a Rotunda Room with "the Onyx Haystack" and lots of geological insight presented by the guide.

MCDOWELL HOUSE AND APOTHECARY

125 South 2nd Street, downtown

Danville 40422

- ❑   Phone: (859) 236-2804. **www.mcdowellhouse.com**
- ❑   Hours: Monday-Saturday 10:00am-Noon & 1:00-4:00pm. Sunday 2:00-4:00pm. Closed Monday (November-February). Closed Thanksgiving, Christmas and winter Mondays.
- ❑   Admission: $7.00 adult, $5.00 senior (62+), $3.00 youth (13-20), $2.00 child (1-12).
- ❑   Tours: Guided 45 minute tours.
- ❑   Note: Gardens with medicinal herbs. Stop over at Constitution Square across the street. FREEBIES: Activity Book - **www.mcdowellhouse.com/mcdowell-childrens-book.pdf**

This medical office is a showcase to one of the world's finest collections of antique apothecary jars and equipment (did you know they used to hide medicine in biscuit dough as the coating?). Danville is the boyhood and adult home of Dr. Ephraim McDowell - the man who performed the world's first successful abdominal surgery.   Jane Todd Crawford, the patient, thought she was pregnant and overdue. After diagnosing a growing ovarian tumor, McDowell suggested her only hope for survival was to travel 60 miles (on horseback) to his office.   After writing a prayer in his journal, he performed the experimental removal on Christmas Day, 1809, while Mrs. Crawford sang hymns. She fully recovered, went home to her family, and lived into her 70s. Just a few of the many very unique items you need to look for are: the clock in the foyer with an arrow hole through it; the cradle that rocks and rolls; the comb-back rocker (if you have long hair you might be chosen to demo this); the little door into the "operating bedroom" with the doctor's tools laid out on the chest of drawers; in the kitchen, an old-fashioned deep fryer (french fries) or "toe" stir (toaster); or why a green jar was always placed within view of the apothecary window. We promise you'll see something here (esp. medically) you've never seen before! Very, very interesting.

PIONEER PLAYHOUSE

840 Stanford Road (US 150)

Danville 40422

❑   Phone: (859) 236-2747. **www.pioneerplayhouse.com**

❑   Hours: Dinner served 7:30pm. Show time 8:30pm. Mid-June to Mid-August. Performances Nightly Tuesday through Saturday.

❑   Admission: Reserved Seats with Dinner & Theatre: around $32.00 (children under 13: $17). Theatre Only: around $18.00 (children under 13: $10)

Operating since the 1950's, this is a rustic style outdoor dinner theatre (in case of rain, indoors). The complex of wooden beam buildings serve as pioneer shops and eateries. Plus, each building tells a unique story about Kentucky history. Seasonally, they perform 5 different plays - usually two of them are rated G - for family audiences (ex. All I Really Need to Know I Learned in Kindergarten or Sherlock Holmes).

GREAT AMERICAN BRASS BAND FESTIVAL

Danville. Centre College Lawn. **www.gabbf.com** "The most prominent and unusual musical festival in the country" is a FREE presentation of world-class bands. Festival highlights include: a balloon race; continuous music beginning Friday evening featuring over a dozen brass bands; a parade; a decorator picnic; fireworks extravaganza. (second weekend in June)

CONSTITUTION SQUARE FESTIVAL

Danville. Constitution Square State Historic Site, downtown. **www.constitutionsquareartsfest.org** Celebrate where Kentucky's Statehood began with a visit to the first Post Office west of the Alleghenies, a jail, the courthouse and the meeting house. The site is set up as life was 200 years ago with arts and crafts demos, living history actors and entertainment. (second weekend in September)

PUMPKIN FESTIVAL

Edmonton. Downtown. Area grown prize pumpkins are weighed, carved and cooked to make fall crafts and food. Monster dance, outhouse race, children's parade. FREE. **www.metcalfechamber.com/events/pumpkin.htm** (first Saturday in October)

OLD STONE JAIL

206 North College Street (downtown, I-65 exit 2)

Bowling Green (Franklin) 42135

- ❑ Phone: (270) 586-4228 **www.simpsoncountykyarchives.com**
- ❑ Hours: Monday-Friday 9:00am-4:00pm, Saturday 10:00am-2:00pm. Central time.

The county's archives are here, but, most probably come to see the graffiti and drawings by Civil War soldiers held in these jailer's quarters. A glimpse at what pioneer justice was like.

LAKE CUMBERLAND STATE RESORT PARK

5465 State Park Road (I-65, exit Cumberland Parkway to US 127 or I-75 exit KY80)

Jamestown 42629

- ❑ Phone: (270) 343-3111 (lodge), (800) 325-1709, (888) 782-8336. **www.lakecumberland.com**

This Park is known throughout the region as one of the finest fishing and pleasure boating areas in the Eastern United States. The Lure Lodge has an indoor swimming pool with exercise room and hot tub and the smaller Pumpkin Creek Lodge is peaceful and quiet. Also available are Wildwood Cottages in the woods, nature trails, horseback riding, campground, marina, rental boats, a beach, tennis, mini-golf and recreation programs. Other points of interest in the area are the Russell Springs Visitor Center (270) 866-4333, Waterway Adventures (800) 844-8862 or www.waterway-adventures.com, Wolf Creek Dam Visitor Center (off US 27, open weekdays) and Wolf Creek National Fish Hatchery (US 127 below dam, 7:00am-3:30pm daily).

COUNTRY HAM DAYS

Lebanon. Downtown. **www.hamdays.com** Over 600 hams are prepared to serve with Southern style side dishes. Cloggers, line dances, steam engine show, Pokey Pig Run and entertainment.. Ham & Biscuit eating contest, pig pen relay race. (last full weekend in September)

APPLE FESTIVAL

Liberty.   Casey   County   Fairgrounds. **www.caseycountyapplefestival.org** The world's largest apple pie is complemented by a parade, apple foods, music, contests and fireworks. The show pieces of the festival are the 10-foot giants produced each year. On Wednesday night they bake a 10-foot chocolate cookie followed by a 10-foot pizza on Thursday night, and of course don't forget the 10-foot apple pie baked from scratch and served free to the public on Saturday. (last weekend in Sept.)

BARREN RIVER LAKE STATE PARK RESORT

1149 State Park Rd (I-65 to the Cumberland Pkwy, then US 31 E south), **Lucas** 42156

❑   Phone: (270) 646-2151 Lodge, (800) 325-0057 reservations, (270) 646-2357 Marina.
       http://parks.ky.gov/parks/resortparks/barren-river/default.aspx

The gently rolling hills of trees now cover the "barren" days when pioneers came to the area and found all vegetation burned away by Indians to promote grassland for grazing buffalo. The lodge, full-service restaurant and cottages curve around the 10,000 acre lake with ample fishing, boating, horseback riding, swimming (pool & beach), hiking, tennis and caving nearby.

GLASGOW HIGHLAND GAMES Barren River Lake SRP. **www.glasgowhighlandgames.com** A Scottish Heritage and Family Celebration with dancing, bagpipe and harp competition, sheepdog demos, and children's games. Tickets for many events. (weekend after Memorial Day - Thursday-Sunday)

MILL SPRINGS BATTLEFIELD
KY 80W

Nancy 42544

- ❑ Phone: (606) 636-4045. **www.millsprings.net**
- ❑ Hours: Dawn to dusk. Visitor Ctr & Museum: Tuesday-Saturday 10am-4pm, Sunday Noon-4pm. Best to tour on weekends.
- ❑ Admission: $5.00 per person. $12.00 per family.
- ❑ Note: Gift shop open weekends esp. during the summer. Nearby in Monticello, Mill Springs Park where an 1840 mill still grinds cornmeal powered by a 40 foot overshot wheel. Open daily 9:00am-5:00pm,. Demos on weekends at 2:00pm (Memorial Day-Labor Day). (606) 368-8189.

Pick up the 9 stop driving or walking tour brochure as you enter the property. This is the site of the 1862 Civil War battle where Confederate General Zollicoffer fell and 203 soldiers died. See both Union and Confederate cemeteries, the area where infantry formed for bayonet charges, and the site of the Confederate field hospital. Combat on the Cumberland is the exhibit featuring the battle interpretation.

PERRYVILLE BATTLEFIELD STATE HISTORIC SITE
1825 Battlefield Road
(US 68 west to US 150 west to SRKY 1920 north)

Perryville 40468

- ❑ Phone: (859) 332-8631 **http://perryvillebattlefield.org**
- ❑ Hours: Park open year-round 9:00am-9:00pm. Museum: 9:00am-5:00pm (April-October). By appointment (November-March).
- ❑ Admission: $1.00-$2.00 per person (age 6+).
- ❑ Note: Picnicking, Gift Shop.

"I think to lose Kentucky is nearly the same as to lose the whole game…", says Lincoln. On October 8, 1862 the tranquil countryside of the area was thundered by cannon explosions and the death of more than 6000 killed, wounded, or missing. The Confederate Cemetery is where many were buried by neighbors and farmers in mounds. Perryville became the site of the most destructive Civil War battle in the state. The Museum tells the details of the battle that was the south's last serious attempt to gain possession of Kentucky. They use many actual maps, cannons from battle, uniforms and weapons to tell the story. There's also a self-guided walking tour of the battlefield park (about one mile long).

PERRYVILLE BATTLEFIELD COMMEMORATION Perryville Battlefield SHS. Living history exhibits and battle re-enactments honor the worst of Kentucky's Civil War battles with encampments, sutters and music. Parking fee. (first full weekend in October)

WILLIAM WHITLEY HOUSE STATE HISTORIC SITE

625 William Whitley Road (US 27 south to US 150 east)

Stanford 40484

❑ Phone: (606) 355-2881
   http://parks.ky.gov/parks/historicsites/william-whitley/default.aspx
❑ Hours: Wednesday-Saturday 9:00am-5:00pm, Sunday 11am-5pm (May thru October).
❑ Admission: $3.00-$5.00 per person.

Mr. Whitley built the first brick house in Kentucky later named "Guardian of Wilderness Road" and had many famous visitors like George Rogers Clark and Daniel Boone. William Whitley is also noted for building the first circular track. As an expression of his anti-British sentiment, he laid his race course on clay vs. grass and ran horses counter-clockwise. While in the house, look for the concealed secret passageway used for escape should the house be invaded by Indians.

PIONEER CHRISTMAS CANDLELIGHT Whitley House State Historic Site. Open house with holiday décor, music and refreshments. Admission. (December weekend)

BIG SOUTH FORK NATIONAL RIVER AND RECREATION AREA

300 Wilburn K Ross Highway (I-75 exit 11. (KY92). I-65 to
Cumberland Pkwy. To US 27, then KY 92 west). Get map to area
from Visitor's Center.

Stearns 42647

- ❏   Phone: (606) 376-5652 Blue Heron. **www.nps.gov/biso**
- ❏   Hours: Visitors Center Saturday-Sunday 9am-5pm (Memorial
  Day weekend to Labor Day weekend). Blue Heron open 9:30am-
  3:30pm daily (April-October). Eastern Time.
- ❏   Admission: FREE
- ❏   Note: Campgrounds, 150 miles of Hiking, 170 miles of Horse
  Trails, Picnicking, Fishing, Mountain Biking, Canoeing,
  Swimming, Boating. Yahoo Falls - Kentucky tallest falls
  accessed by car on KY 700. Educators:
  www.nps.gov/biso/forteachers/index.htm (teachers guides)

The park encompasses 119,000 acres of wilderness, rivers and
back country scattered with spectacular gorges and bluffs. Sparsely
settled but once logged, you'll see remnants of industry. The Blue
Heron Coal Mining Camp (KY 742 off US 27 accessed by car or
railroad) is a must see in the area. Within Mine 18 is the rugged
and isolated life of a mining community which operated from 1938
to 1962 and employed 300 people. Recorded voices of the people
who actually lived and worked in the village tell their story from
inside "shell structures" representing simple homes, a church, a
school, a bathhouse and a company store that even sold jewelry.
The workers were paid in script, not cash, so they had to buy
everything at the company store. The Tram bridge and tipple
remain - also the entrance to the mine is open and an explanation
of the process is given. This is a wonderfully educational,
imaginative way to study the lives of miners.

BIG SOUTH FORK SCENIC RAILWAY

21 Main Street (Parkway to US 27 south to SRKY 92 west)

Stearns 42647

- ❏   Phone: (606) 376-5330 or (800) GO-ALONG

For updates visit our website: www.kidslovetravel.com

www.bsfsry.com

- ❑ Admission: $25.25 adult, $23.75 senior (60+), $15.50 child (3-12). Add about $10 for lunch.
- ❑ Tour Departure: Wednesday, Thursday, Friday at 10:00am & 11:00am. Weekends at 11:00am and 2:30pm (April-November)
- ❑ Note: Whistle Stop Café, Sterns Restaurant (Coal Miners Special - pinto beans and corn bread). The McCreary County Museum of history is also in this complex. The Barthell Mining Camp is an optional train ride to an old, restored mining town with an overnight in a miner's cabin (606-376-8749).

A scenic ride to Blue Heron aboard open-sided or enclosed rail cars that are pulled thru steep-walled canyons and alongside streams, pass thru a tunnel and over a bridge and into the Big South Fork River valley. Board the train at the newly restored freight warehouse (a restaurant and gift shop inside) where you can usually hear live music. The Kentucky & Tennessee Railway at one time serviced as the primary passage not only for timber and coal coming out of the valley, but also for the workers and supplies going into the coal and lumber camps. This is the best way to visit the stopover place - the Blue Heron Coal Camp.

OLD MULKEY MEETINGHOUSE STATE HISTORIC SITE

38 Old Mulkey Road (KY 1446 south off KY 100 OR KY 90 to KY 163)

Tompkinsville 42167

- ❑ Phone: (270) 487-8481
  www.stateparks.com/old_mulkey_meeting_house.html
- ❑ Hours: Daily 9:00am-5:00pm.
- ❑ Admission: FREE, self-guided tours.

Built in 1804, this is the oldest log meetinghouse in Kentucky. Many Revolutionary War soldiers and pioneers, including Daniel Boone's sister, Hannah, are buried in the church cemetery. Built during a period of religious revival, the structure has 12 corners in the shape of a cross and three doors, symbolic of the Holy Trinity.

The Southeast Chapter at a Glance...

Barbourville
- Dr. Thomas Walker

Beattyville
- Wooly Worm Fest

Benham
- Ky Coal Mining
- Portal 31 Mine

Berea
- Berea College Craft
- Boone Tavern
- Berea Craft Fest
- Spoonbread Fest

Breaks
- Breaks Interstate Pk

Buckhorn
- Buckhorn Lake St Resort Pk

Corbin
- Cumberland Falls St Resort Pk
- Cumberland Falls St Pk Lodge
- Harland Sanders Café/ Museum

Cumberland
- Kingdom Come Pk

Elkhorn City
- Elkhorn City Railrd

Frakes/Harlan/Hindman/Hyden
- Henderson Sttlemnt
- Pine Mtn Settlemnt
- Hindman School
- Frontier Nursing

London
- Levi Jackson Wilderness
- World Chicken Fest
- Camp Wildcat

Middlesboro
- Cumberland Gap Natl Historic Pk

Paintsville
- Mountain Homeplace
- Paintsville Lake St Pk
- Ky Apple Fest

Pinesville
- Pine Mtn St Resort Pk

Pikeville
- Hillbilly Days Fest
- Hatfield & McCoy Fest

Prestonsburg
- Jenny Wiley Park Theatre
- Ky Opry
- Battle Middle Crk

Renfro Valley
- Ky Music Hall of Fame
- Renfro Valley Entertainment

Richmond
- Fort Boonesborough
- Hummel Planetarium
- Civil War Driving Tour
- Whitehall Historic Site

Sassafras
- Carr Creek St Pk

Slade
- Ky Reptile Zoo
- Natural Bridge

Whitesburg
- Appalshop

Williamsburg
- Ky Splash WaterPk

Chapter 4
Area - South East (SE)

Our Favorites...

* Berea College Log House - Berea
* Cumberland Falls State Park Resort Park - Corbin
* Harland Sander's Cafe & Museum - Corbin
* Mountain Homeplace - Paintsville
* Bybee Pottery - Richmond
* Ft. Boonesborough State Park - Richmond
* Hummel Planterium (EKU) - Richmond
* Natural Bridge - Slade

"In Awe"
- Natural Bridge

*A QUICK TOUR OFF SOUTHEASTERN KENTUCKY
HIGHWAYS & PARKWAYS...*

Driving through Lexington and just south on I-75 (exit 95), we
come upon another town full of intriguing sites. Richmond is
home the Hummel Planetarium and Space Theater (Eastern
Kentucky University) with many family shows stimulating the
night sky with over 10,000 stars, multiple projections of five
planets, a sun, a moon, etc – all of these operating simultaneously
with surround sound. Richmond has a driving Civil War Tour, a
nice stop at Fort Boonesborough, and the home of Cassius
Marcellus Clay (a fervent emancipationist and friend to Abraham
Lincoln), White Hall State Historic Site. The home is rather
progressive for it's time...they had running water and central
heating (look for hidden outlets).

Now that we're talking about pottery, let's visit the craft capital of
Kentucky – Berea (exit 76). They've been making brooms here for
80 years and weaving even longer. Visit the working studios of
woodworkers, weavers (several students work together to make
one piece-it takes two hours just to string the loom), furniture
makers and broom craft. The tours are well worth the time and
you'll find lots of questions to ask as you go along.

Our last stop down I-75 is Corbin (exit 29). Two of the most
unique sites in Kentucky are here. Take a side trip around
lunchtime at the Harland Sanders Café and Museum and "Eat
where it all began"! See the Colonel's kitchen as it was in 1940
(early dishwashers, French fry press) when he developed his secret
recipe. Now, purchase some KFC fast food and munch on it sitting
next to a statue of Colonel Sanders.

Also in Corbin is the site of the famous moonbow (arch of light
and colors), a phenomenon not found anywhere else in the Western
Hemisphere! Cumberland Falls State Park, the "Niagara of the
South" is a 125-foot wide curtain of water falling 60 feet –
dramatic night and day. To try to catch the moonbow, it is best to
visit at night when there's a full moon. The museum, lodge and
hiking trails are all "family-friendly" and worth an overnight stay.

As you travel east on the Mountain Parkway, be sure to stop in Slade at Natural Bridge State Resort Park. It's probably worth an overnight here because the lodge hosts cookouts, square dances and special hikes and camps. Caves, rocks, gulches, mines and gorges are strewn throughout but the best "WOW" is Natural Bridge. It's truly amazing to hike or chairlift (sloped gently at first, then a sharp steep climb up the final stretch!) up to the bridge. A natural sandstone arch, the bridge spans 78 feet long and 65 feet high. There are no guardrails and everyone can walk right across that high bridge, then finish the trail past scenic overlooks and narrow paths (Fat Man's Misery) that lead under the bridge. The whole experience is like a giant outdoor amusement ride.

Take the Mountain Parkway all the way east to Paintsville as you continue your Appalachian adventure at Mountain Homeplace. Trained guides in period clothing demo skills and crafts – most activities are centuries old. The Farmhouse and The Church were centers of family life. In the one-room schoolhouse, you better behave so you don't get the "board of education". Before you tour, be sure to watch an informative introduction movie "The Land of Tomorrow" – narrated by actor Richard Thomas whose ancestral roots are linked to the area.

On your way back up to Prestonsburg, a great autumn hike is through Breaks Interstate Park, the "Grand Canyon of the South". This is the largest canyon east of the Mississippi, over 5 miles long, 1600 feet deep and surrounded by sheer vertical cliffs. A Visitor's Center has natural science and historical artifacts along with demos of the areas formations. Camp or lodge and check out Laurel Lake, caves, hidden springs and falls and rapids.

Jenny Wiley is the name associated with Prestonsburg. In the State Park by the same name, take the Skylift 4700 feet to the top of Sugar Camp Mountain or wander thru the Nature Center. Wiley endured the loss of her children and brothers during an Indian invasion. Jenny was taken captive and later escaped to start a new family.

DR. THOMAS WALKER STATE HISTORIC SITE

HC 89 Box 1868/ KY 459 (I-75 exit 29, south on US 25E)

Barbourville 40906

❑   Phone: (606) 546-4400

    http://parks.ky.gov/parks/historicsites/thomas-walker/default.aspx

❑   Hours: Daily 9:00am-9:30pm (April-October)

Dr. Thomas Walker was, in fact, the first frontiersman headed into Kentucky (he led the first expedition through Cumberland Gap in 1750). A physician and surveyor, he named the Cumberland and built a cabin, a replica of which stands on the site today. There's a gift shop and mini-golf on site, too. FREE admission.

WOOLY WORM FESTIVAL

Beattyville. Downtown. A unique annual celebration of the predictor of coming winter weather with announcement of results of a survey sent to the National Weather Service along with crafts, entertainment and a wooly worm race (as the fans cheer them on!). (third weekend in October)

KENTUCKY COAL MINING MUSEUM

KY 160 - Main Street, **Benham 40807**

❑   Phone: (606) 848-1530   **www.kingdomcome.org/museum/**

❑   Hours: Tuesday-Saturday 10:00am-5:00pm. Closed Holidays.

❑   Admission: $3-$6.00 per person.

❑   Note: Across the street is the School House Inn & Restaurant (606) 848-3000. Home-cooked food served in a historic coal camp school.

The building is the original coal company's commissary - now full of memorabilia from early coal mining days. Some considered camps in this area of Kentucky "Cadillac" compared to others in the coal region - mostly because miners were treated with the respect and dignity they deserved. A guided or self-guided tour gives you a feel for what it was like to live, play, and mostly, work

KY COAL MINING MUSEUM (continued)

at this unique coal camp. The museum's newest exhibit is the "Mock Mine - a short walk winding along coal corridors" with vivid sound and video from modern mines. Many like the exhibits of a typical company hospital, a typical miner's home, the mock mine and the tribute to Loretta Lynn, the "Coal Miner's Daughter" (with permission and personal artifacts from Loretta herself).

PORTAL 31 TOUR

US 160 (2 miles east of Benham)

Benham (Lynch) 40855

- ❑　Phone: (606) 848-1530
- ❑　Hours: Tuesday-Saturday 9am-5pm
- ❑　Admission: $5.-$10 for tram tours.

An outdoors tour of the 1920 coal mine and buildings. The walking tour includes the 1920 coal tipple (small-size "train conveyor" - the largest in the world at that time), the Lamp House (where miners checked in and picked up lights and mine numbers), the original post office, a depot, school, firehouse and, best of all, the mine portal entrance and actually into the mine.

The underground tram tour with animated characters gives insights into the lives and fears of coal miners in the 1900s. Built by US Steel, it was once the largest coal camp in the world with 1000+ structures.

BEREA COLLEGE CRAFTS ON THE SQUARE & LOG HOUSE

College Square (I-75 exit 76)

Berea 40403

- ❑　Phone: (800) 347-3892　　**www.bereacollegecrafts.com**
- ❑　Hours: Monday-Saturday 8:00am-6:00pm, Sunday 1:00-5:00pm (April-December). Extended summer hours.
- ❑　Admission: FREE
- ❑　Tours: Walk along the Square as storefront studios invite you to enter and watch and ask questions of students crafting..

All students of this college work on campus in lieu of paying tuition and board - their crafts are featured at this gallery. They've been making brooms here for 80 years and weaving even longer! Visit the working studios of woodworkers (see them make the famous "Berea Basket" with all wood and paper product used), weavers (several students will make one piece - it takes two hours just to string the loom), furniture makers and broom craft (use the stalk and husk of "broom corn" - see a broom made before your eyes, then purchase it if you like). Master craftsmen supervise and teach. We were very impressed with the school's philosophies and

students' attitudes about work and study! The tours are well worth the time and you'll find lots of questions to ask as you go along.

BOONE TAVERN: Combine crafts in town with helpings of traditional Kentucky fare at Boone Tavern restaurant operated by the college's student industries since 1909. Signature items include spoonbread, Chicken Flakes in Bird's Nest (creamed chicken served in a crisp basket of fried potatoes) or maybe try some black-eyed peas, fried green tomatoes or corn pudding. The slightly formal furnishings mean children should be on their best behavior. Entrees start at $8.00 with children's portion pricing - may we suggest, lunchtime is best. (**www.boonetavernhotel.com**)

BEREA CRAFT FESTIVAL

Berea. Throughout downtown & Indian Fort Theatre. Voted the top 20 events in the southeast, there are usually over 125 artists from around the country demonstrating and selling their workmanship. International music, dance and theater are a wonderful compliment. Food and family activities. **Www.bereacraftfestival.com** Admission (over 12) (mid-July weekend)

SPOONBREAD FESTIVAL

Berea. Memorial Park, Jefferson St. This festival honors the famous bread served at Boone Tavern. Check out the spoonbread eating contest, live music, children's activities, food and hot air balloons. **www.spoonbreadfestival.com** (second weekend in September)

BREAKS INTERSTATE PARK

PO Box 100 (south of Pikeville on KY/ VA 80)

Breaks 24607

- ❑ Phone: (540) 865-4413 or (540) 865-4414 or (800) 982-5122 **www.breakspark.com**
- ❑ Hours: Park open 7:30am – 11:30pm except Winter when it's open until 6:00 pm. Visitor's Center open 10:00am-6:00pm seasonally.(April-October)
- ❑ Note: Sheltowee Trace Outfitters (800) 541-RAFT. Elkhorn Adventures Whitewater Rafting (606) 754-5080.

Sometimes called the "Grand Canyon of the South", this is the largest canyon east of the Mississippi; over 5-miles long, 1600 feet deep surrounded by sheer vertical cliffs! A paved road leads to the entrance of the canyon rim and there's a Visitor Center with natural science and historical artifacts and demos of the area's formation. Check out the park's Laurel Lake, caves, hidden springs and Russell Fork River's falls and rapids. Hiking and rafting are the name of the game here. Also within the park is a lodge, cottages, campgrounds and a Splash in the Park mini-waterpark (seasonal-fee charged).

Throughout much of the year, you'll find demonstrations of a working gristmill adjacent to the park Visitor Center. The gristmill—an original gas-powered model dating back to the 1930s—grinds corn into corn meal.

BUCKHORN LAKE STATE RESORT PARK

4441 Kentucky Highway 1833 (I-64 east to the Mountain Parkway, exit Campton and take KY 15 south to KY 28 west, then KY 1833)

Buckhorn 41721

❑   Phone: (606) 398-7510 or (606) 398-7382 (log church)
      http://parks.ky.gov/parks/resortparks/buckhorn-lake/default.aspx

Getting away from it all is easy here especially for nature-lovers, fishermen and hikers. When staying at the lodge, you can easily hike down to Moonshiner Hollow to the 1200 acre mountain lake below the path. Many slowly make their way down there after dinner in the lodge or they curl up with a good book or magazine by the copper-hooded fireplace in the lodge's lounging area. Maybe you want to make a side trip to Buckhorn Log Church built in 1927. Its large pipe organ and natural white oak interior make it a man-made natural beauty too (open 9:00am-5:00pm daily). Check out their cottages, marina, rental boats, pool, beach, horseback riding trails and tennis and recreation programs.

CUMBERLAND FALLS STATE RESORT PARK

7351 State Route 90 (I-75 exit Corbin to US 25W, then to SRKY 90), **Corbin 40701**

❑   Phone: (606)528-4121 or (800) 325-0063 reservations
      http://parks.ky.gov/parks/resortparks/cumberland-falls/default.aspx

❑   Hours: 6:00am-Midnight. Until 3:00am the 2 days before, after and including a full moon. Eastern Time.

❑   Admission: FREE. Charge for boat rides or rentals.

❑   Tours: Rainbow Mist Ride to the Base of Falls (mid-May thru Labor Day).

- ❏ Sheltowee Trace Outfitters raft trips (800) 541-RAFT or **www.ky-rafting.com**
- ❏ Note: Dupont Lodge with dining, Cottages, Campground, Gift Shop, Pool, Horseback Riding, Tennis, Picnicking, Rafting, geocaching trips.

The "Niagara of the South" is a 125 foot wide curtain of water falling 60 feet - dramatic night and day. But, the accomplishment is to have been touched by a moonbow! (Moonbow Dates listed on website) Finally, we arranged an overnight so we and a few

hundred others, could walk in the quiet, moonlit night (about 8:45pm) towards the Falls. After a few seconds stare . . . we captured the white spray arch that then turned into a rainbow of color the longer you watched. How outstanding and romantic (esp. for night owls)! Dawn to dusk viewing is better for photos and safety.

Eagle Falls are nearby and are a beautifully high stream of water (vs. a roaring gush). There's also a Nature Preserve and the Moonbow Trail connects to the Daniel Boone National Forest.

We find many families like to stay overnight at the lodge (very family friendly with family activities throughout the first floor Great Room area) and wander or hike in the daytime. The Falls are within long walking distance for grade-schoolers and strollers, but there are some hills.

DID YOU KNOW? The famous moonbow (a rainbow arch of light and colors best during a full moon), is a phenomena not found anywhere else in the Western Hemisphere!

CUMBERLAND FALLS STATE RESORT PARK LODGE

7351 State Route 90 (I-75 exit Corbin to US 25W, then to SRKY 90), **Corbin** 40701

❑   Phone: (800) 325-0063 reservations

http://parks.ky.gov/parks/resortparks/cumberland-falls/default.aspx

Now, off to the Lodge. Solid hemlock beams and knotty pine paneling complement the massive stone fireplaces. The rooms have been updated and their rates begin at ~$63.00! The buffet offers classic southern dishes and there is a reasonable a la carte menu. Our favorite memory is playing ping-pong and checkers while other families sat around and played cards. Visit the gift shop, featuring a large selection of Kentucky handcrafts and souvenirs. There's also a snack shop and visitors center, both located in the falls area. Inside the center, a three-dimension map outlines major park facilities. Other exhibits show the area's history and illustrates Native American life. Guided tours (30 minutes long) leave from the Center most weekends and summer days. You can also rent one and two-bedroom cottages, most with fireplaces.

HARLAND SANDERS CAFÉ & MUSEUM

US 25W (I-75 exit 29, US 25E south to US 25W)

Corbin 40701

❑   Phone: (606) 528-2163
      www.corbinkycityguide.com/kfc/kfc.htm
❑   Hours: Open daily 10:00am-10:00pm.
❑   Admission: FREE

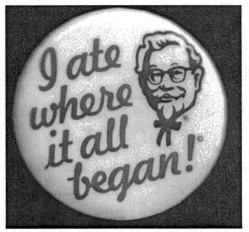

Eat where it all began! The original Kentucky Fried Chicken Restaurant serves KFC products in the large restored dining room. See the Colonel's kitchen as it was in 1940 (early dishwashers, french fry press) when he developed his secret recipe. The business flourished because he combined good cooking, hard work and showmanship. Be sure to look in the display case for the cooking clock with the third hand. Also see his office, model motel room he rented and much of his marketing strategies. Do you know how many herbs and spices are in his chicken recipe? Did you know it was his honor system franchise concept (that he sold across country) that, at age 65+, made him money - and not his own restaurant?

KINGDOM COME STATE PARK

Box M (off US 119N)

Cumberland 40823

❑ Phone: (606) 589-2479

http://parks.ky.gov/parks/recreationparks/kingdom-come/default.aspx

This is Kentucky's highest state park on the crest of Pine Mountain. The park's name was taken from John Fox Jr.'s famous novel "The Little Shepherd of Kingdom Come" a book about an orphaned youth and his journey through the hills and into the Civil War. This book was the first book to sell one million copies. If you like nature, you will love seeing unusual rock formations like Log Rock, a natural sandstone bridge, and Raven Rock, a 290 foot rock at a 45-degree angle. The popular Little Shepherd Trail (Harlan to Winterburg) is recommended for hikers and slow vehicles. There's a campground, pedal boats and 5 miles of hiking trails.

ELKHORN CITY RAILROAD MUSEUM

100 Pine Street

Elkhorn City 41522

❑ Phone: (606) 754-8300 **http://elkhorncityrrm.tripod.com**
❑ Hours: Tuesday - Saturday 10:00am-4:00pm. Sunday Noon-4pm. (closed winter months)
❑ Admission: Donations

See how the railroad made its way into the area with photos, tools, uniforms, and instruments used on the railroad. Speak to retired railroad employees on the history of the railroad locally.

HENDERSON SETTLEMENT

KY 90 (16 miles southwest of Pineville)

Frakes 40940

- ❑   Phone: (606) 337-3613 **http://hendersonsettlement.com**
- ❑   Hours: Craft shop Monday-Friday 8:00-4:30, Saturday by appointment.
- ❑   Tours: 8:30am, 10:00am, 1:00pm & 3:00pm. Prefer by appointment or as part of a mission work group.

Henderson was one of a number of settlement schools developed in rural areas, particularly in Appalachia, as a Progressive Era solution to poverty, isolation, and lack of opportunity. The schools, with boarding facilities for students whose homes were too distant for daily travel, clustered with community services, offered training for various trades, and often became laboratories for the study and preservation of local crafts and traditions. Tours of the 1,300-acre mission include the demonstration farm, with its greenhouse, orchards and vegetable gardens.

PINE MOUNTAIN SETTLEMENT

36 KY 510 (at KY 221 & KY 510)

Harlan 40831

- ❑   Phone: (606) 558-3571
  www.pinemountainsettlementschool.com

Nestled in the mountains near Harlan, 800 acres of forests and fields invite you to learn folklore and the heritage of this settlement school through hands-on courses. Local mountain craftsmen help you make and take home treasures. Native stone and wood buildings provide a beautiful setting for a retreat.

HINDMAN SETTLEMENT SCHOOL

KY 160 (off KY 80 one mile)

Hindman 41822

- ❑   Phone: (606) 785-5475. **www.hindmansettlement.org**
- ❑   Hours: Monday-Friday 8:00am-5:00pm
- ❑   Admission: FREE

Hindman Settlement School was founded in 1902 on the forks of Troublesome Creek. In addition to Hindman Settlement School, Hindman offers the Appalachian Artisan Center and Café, Working Artisans, the Kentucky School of Craft and the Marie Stewart Museum & Crafts Shop. Folk dance evenings and workshops on Appalachian culture are offered. A 12 minute video is shown on the history of the school.

Hindman is also home to the annual Gingerbread Festival which takes place in September. Knott County, known as the "Elk Capitol of the East," also has lots to offer, including: Elk tours and an elk viewing station near Sutton Memorial Park.

FRONTIER NURSING SERVICE

KY 80 (US 421 off Daniel Boone Pkwy.)

Hyden 41749

❑ Phone: (606) 672-2317. **www.frontier.edu/about-frontier/frontier-nursing-service**

❑ Hours: By Appointment.

Up until the 1930s, an American woman was more likely to die in childbirth than from any other disease, except tuberculosis. The mortality rate was particularly high for pregnant women in rural areas where hospitals and qualified medical care were scarce. Breckinridge recognized this concern and succeeded in one of the pioneering attempts to bring professionalized health care to rural-America. At the oldest school of nurse-midwifery (est. 1925) you'll see the Mary Breckenridge Hospital and nursing schools and centers.

Tours: With a little advance notice, we can arrange individual and group tours of the historic headquarters of the Frontier Nursing Service at Wendover and the Frontier Nursing University. Your tours includes: a visit to the FNS Historic Photo Gallery located in the Garden House, a viewing of the Forgotten Frontier, a film made by Mary Breckinridge's cousin, Marvin Breckinridge in 1930, a visit to Mary Breckinridge's home, the Big House, a delicious home-cooked lunch in the Dog Trot Dining room of the Big House and a relaxing stroll down the Hurricane Trail.

After a short drive to Hospital Hill, the tour continues at the former Hyden Hospital location, which is now the home of the Frontier Nursing University. While at the University, visitors will see the St. Christopher's Chapel featuring a 15th century English stained glass window, and the Haggin Dorm with a brick from Florence Nightingale's home located on the second floor.

The price for lunch is $8.00 per person and they can accommodate groups up to 15 people. Please call (606) 672-2317 to make your reservations.

LEVI JACKSON WILDERNESS ROAD STATE PARK

998 Levi Jackson Mill Road (I-75 exit 38)

London 40744

- ❑   Phone: (606) 878-8000

    http://parks.ky.gov/parks/recreationparks/levi-jackson/default.aspx
- ❑   Hours: Park open 24 hours. Mill grounds open 8:00am-4:30pm in the summer. Museum open daily 9am-4:30pm (April-October). Everything closed the week of Christmas.
- ❑   Admission: FREE. Seasonal pool & mini-golf charge admission.
- ❑   Note: Campground, Gift Shop, Pool (nice, w/ two water slides and a children's pool), Mini-golf, Picnicking, & Archery range.

Begin with historic trails - the Wilderness Road (30 foot wide wagon road used by pioneers) and Boone's Trace. Over 200,000 eastern settlers forged into KY wilderness between 1774 and 1796 for the promise of fertile land, abundant game, clear streams and rivers. They faced many dangers - McNitt's Defeat (worst KY Indian massacre) occurred here on the Wilderness Road in 1796. The Mountain Life Museum is a log building with pioneer artifacts such as kitchen utensils, weapons and furniture. At McHargue's Mill you'll see a working reproduction mill dating back to the late 1700s with authentic interior works. "The people went and gathered it and ground it in mill" - Numbers 11:8.

DID YOU KNOW? you can see the largest display of millstones in the country.

WORLD CHICKEN FESTIVAL

London. Downtown. **www.chickenfestival.com** You are egg-spected for this good time complete with a gander at the World's Largest Skillet, entertainment and rides. It celebrates the county where the first Kentucky Fried Chicken was established. Come with an appetite! (last full weekend in September - Thursday-Sunday)

CAMP WILDCAT RE-ENACTMENT

London. Wildcat Mountain. The Civil War battle of Wildcat is re-enacted as the first Union victory of the War (along Wilderness Road) with living history exhibits. **www.wildcatreenactment.org** (third weekend in October)

CUMBERLAND GAP NATIONAL HISTORICAL PARK

PO Box 1848 (I-75 exit US 25E south 50 miles)

Middlesboro 40965

- ❏ Phone: (606) 248-2817. **www.nps.gov/cuga/**
- ❏ Hours: Visitor's Center 8:00-5:00 daily except winter hours 9am-4pm. Park open 'til dusk.
- ❏ Admission: FREE
- ❏ Tours: Gap Cave Tours are $8 adult, $4 child (5-12) and seniors. Hensley Settlement Tours are $5-$10.

Go back in time when the gap - a natural passage through the mountain barrier - had been used by Indians, and then discovered by explorer Dr. Thomas Walker. Daniel Boone and John Finley followed in 1769 - Boone and his axmen making the first Kentucky trail named the Wilderness Road. By the late 1700's, over 10,000 settlers had come west through the Cumberland Gap. The park is the largest National Historical Park in the country with over 20,000 acres. Start by viewing the orientation programs available at the Visitor Center. Look over the pictures here and then see for yourself the Pinnacle Overlook (panoramic view of three states) or Fort McCook (built by Confederate forces to guard the gap during the Civil War). There's a Pioneer playhouse for the kids to romp in.

A hiker's paradise - 80% of the park has unpaved roads (be sure to check the length and difficulty of trails - stick to nature trails close to paved roads for the kids). The Wilderness Road Campground has 160 campsites for tents or RVs, a restored log cabin at Martin's Fork (a Kentucky Wild River), and all day hike or 4 hour shuttle tour to the Hensley Settlement (a restored Appalachian community that flourished in isolation years ago - guided tours - if your family has endurance of the all-day hiking or several hours of driving to get there).

MOUNTAIN HOMEPLACE

(US 23 to SRKY 40 west to SR 2275 north, near Paintsville Lake)

Paintsville 41240

❑   Phone: (606) 297-1850 or (800) 542-5790 Tourism
     www.mountainhomeplace.com
❑   Hours: Tuesday-Saturday 8:30am-5:00pm (April – October).
❑   Admission: $6.00 adult, $5.00 senior (55+), $4.00 child (6-17).
❑   Note: Gift Shop and Crafts Store and an Auditorium. Before you tour, be sure to watch an informative introduction movie "The Land of Tomorrow" - narrated by the famous actor Richard Thomas whose ancestral roots are linked to the area. Many structures here are original.

Trained guides in period clothing demo skills and crafts - most activities are centuries old. The family farm area has giant oxen, goats, pigs, and chickens. The farm house was the center of family life and everything was self-contained. They grew crops and raised animals for food and crafted their housewares. The Church was the center of early pioneer settlements and the hard-working families took time out each month to gather and share and nurture one another. In the one-room schoolhouse you better behave so you don't get the "board of education". The blacksmith shop has "horse-tails" to tell. Did you know there were no outhouses and no toilet paper around in those days? Pick you favorite tree, mark it and find a nice big leaf! You'll soon discover these simple, harsh lives were only happy through worship and music. Impromptu concerts on the porch are easy to spot - just listen to the "pickers and grinners" playing music from the hills.

PAINTSVILLE LAKE STATE PARK

PO Box 726 (US 460 off KY 40), **Paintsville 41240**

❑   Phone: (606) 297-5253

http://parks.ky.gov/parks/recreationparks/paintsville-lake/default.aspx

Lots of water for boating, skiing and fishing at yet another state park with abundant water areas. Along the 1140 acres of lake are wooded coves and steep cliffs that provide the background scenery for pristine water activities. There's a full service marina with rental houseboats, pontoons and fishing boats too.

KENTUCKY APPLE FESTIVAL

Paintsville. Downtown. The orchards are harvested and the products honored with apple foods and crafts, amusement rides, a parade, square dancing and clogging and live entertainment. Fried apple pies are a must try. **www.kyapplefest.org** (first week in October)

HILLBILLY DAYS FESTIVAL

Pikeville. Downtown. More than 60,000 people will show up for a fun look at the Hillbilly stereotype with food, a carnival, a parade and music that puts everyone in a "laid back" kind of mood. **Www.hillbillydays.com** (mid-April for three days)

HATFIELD & MCCOY FESTIVAL

Pikeville. Downtown. Light-hearted joking and fun surround the most famous feud in history. McCoys from all over the world and their invited guests (The Hatfields) celebrate together. To make it a true contest, a marathon is held. WHO WON THE FEUD, the Hatfield's or the McCoys? At the end of the race, the family with the lowest total time will win the feud. (second Saturday in June)

PINE MOUNTAIN STATE RESORT PARK

1050 State Park Road (off US 25E)

Pineville 40977

❑   Phone: (606) 337-3066 or (800) 325-1712
      **http://parks.ky.gov/parks/resortparks/pine-
      mountain/default.aspx**

With 27 miles of trails leading through the valleys of the Kentucky
Ridge State Forest. The trails are so popular, they have been given
names like Hemlock Garden, Little Shepherd, Honeymoon Falls,
Living Stairway and Rock Hotel. Chained Rock is a huge chain
anchored to a boulder that seems to hold it in place. The new Pine
Mountain Trail passes through the park. The resort lodge is on a
mountaintop and cottages are available too. In a natural cove in
the forest lies the Laurel Cove Amphitheater open for
entertainment and festivals. There's also a campground, pool and
mini-golf.

JENNY WILEY STATE RESORT PARK

75 Theatre Court (US 23/460 exit SR 3 east)

Prestonsburg 41653

❑   Phone: (606) 886-2711 or (800) 325-0142 reservations
      **http://parks.ky.gov/parks/resortparks/jenny-
      wiley/default.aspx**
❑   Hours: Open dawn to dusk. Nature Center: Tuesday-Saturday
      8am-4pm.
❑   Admission: Free
❑   Note: Early February is Elk Viewing Tours of the magnificent
      animal. Van tour price is $10-$20.

Ride the Mountain Parkway Skylift on Sugar Camp Mountain
4700 ft. to the top (daily Memorial Day weekend-Labor day,
Weekends in the Spring & Fall). The Nature Center has local
wildlife, native plants, animals and local history. Named for a
brave pioneer woman, Jenny Wiley, who was taken captive by
Indians in 1789. Wiley endured the loss of her children and
brother, yet escaped after eleven months of captivity. She then
started a new family and raised them - living until 72 years old.

Weave thru the trails along Dewey Lake as your family pretends to imagine what a pioneer heroine must have endured.

Lodge with dining room, Cottages, Campground, Gift Shop, Marina with boat launch and rentals, Pool, 10.25 miles of Hiking Trails, Picnicking. The Music Highway Grill serves Kentucky favs like fried catfish, hot browns, country ham and uses locally grown meats and produce when available.

JENNY WILEY THEATRE

121 Theatre Court (US 23/460 exit SR 3 east -in Jenny Wiley State Resort Park), **Prestonsburg** 41653

❑   Phone: (606) 886-9274 or (877) CALL-JWT
       www.jwtheatre.com
❑   Hours: Tuesday-Sunday, mid-June to mid-August. Evening
       outdoor performance begins at 8:15 pm, doors open at 7:30 pm.
❑   Admission: $11.00-$22.00.

Broadway musicals (ex.Peter Pan) and the story of "The Legend of Jenny Wiley" (performed two dates each summer).

KENTUCKY OPRY

Performances at the Mountain Arts Center (off US 23 South)

Prestonsburg 41653

❑   Phone: (606) 886-2623 or (888) 622-2787
       www.macarts.com

Family entertainment with programs of country, bluegrass, pop and gospel year-round. Look for "Munroe" the goofy character that is trying to get into showbiz or look for performances by students called Junior Pros.

BATTLE OF MIDDLE CREEK

Prestonsburg. Middle Creek Natl Battlefield. Future President James A. Garfield commanded the Union troops at this battle on January 10, 1862. It ended up being the largest battle in Eastern Kentucky. Technically a draw, but the Confederate troops retreated. See a re-enactment. **Www.middlecreek.org** (August)

KENTUCKY MUSIC HALL OF FAME AND MUSEUM

2590 Richmond Road (I-75 exit 62, east on Hwy 25)

Renfro Valley 40473

❑ Phone: (606) 256-1000 or (877) 356-3263
www.kentuckymusicmuseum.com
❑ Hours: Wednesday-Saturday 10:00am-6:00pm.
❑ Admission: $7.50 adult, $7.00 senior, $4.50 child (6- 12).

The Hall of Fame includes exhibit cases for artifacts, instruments and costumes of honored inductees. You'll see and hear hundreds of entertainers like...Patty Loveless, Loretta Lynn, Bill Monroe, Rosemary Clooney, Billy Ray Cyrus, Ricky Skaggs and the Judds. Also included in the Museum is an instrument room (visitors touch, hear and perform); a sound booth where you can actually sing and record; and a timeline of Kentucky Music from front porch jamboree to radio to major public event concerts.

RENFRO VALLEY ENTERTAINMENT CENTER

I-75 exit 62 (US 25)

Renfro Valley 40473

❑ Phone: (606) 256-2638 or (800) 765-7464
www.renfrovalley.com
❑ Hours: Afternoon and evening shows. Sunday "Renfro Valley Gatherin'' at 8:30am. Barn Dance on Saturday nights at 7:00pm. Village open March-December.
❑ Admission: Varies with production. Best to get on their mailing list for program offerings.
❑ Note: RV Park. Renfro Valley Lodge Motel & Cabins.

Country music, family comedy and headliner concerts and festivals. "Kentucky's Country Music Capital" has an average of 12 shows weekly, Country restaurants, and Brush Arbor Log Shopping Village.

HARVEST FESTIVAL Renfro Valley. Fall harvest-time with an old fashioned flare including molasses made from a mule-drawn press, antique farm machinery, petting zoo, music and a covered-wagon train. (first weekend in October)

FIDDLERS FESTIVAL Renfro Valley. Toe-tapping fun as fiddlers from around the country get together to perform and just jam. (third or fourth weekend in October)

CHRISTMAS IN THE VALLEY Renfro Valley. One of Kentucky's largest light displays, performances and special holiday shopping. (weekend before Thanksgiving - mid December)

EASTERN KENTUCKY UNIVERSITY
(HUMMEL PLANETARIUM)
Lancaster Avenue (off KY 876)
Richmond 40475

❑ Phone: (859) 622-1000. **www.planetarium.eku.edu/**
❑ Note: You might want to ask the staff a clever question like: Has anyone ever been hit by a meteorite? Like to look at the sky online, go to the www.skyviewcafe.com and take a look!

HUMMEL PLANETARIUM AND SPACE THEATER - (859) 622-1547, Kit Carson Drive, Eastern Bypass. The 13th largest planetarium in the US with space science gift shop. Admission around $3.00-$4.00/person. Public Programs Saturdays. A visit to the Hummel Planetarium is a trip through the universe. Planetarium equipment is used to stimulate the night sky consists of a giant star ball with the capacity of projecting over 10,000 stars, multiple projections of five planets, a sun, the moon, etc. - all of these operating simultaneously with surround sound. You can also travel throughout space and see the planets from other planets besides earth. At the end of each program, see the KY night sky as it will look that night - look for your favorite constellations.

MEADOWBROOK FARM PROGRAM - (859) 622-1310. Meadowbrook Road (off KY 52). Agricultural production, dairy cattle, beef cattle, sheep, swine and cropping operations. Welcome during normal business hours or tours by appointment.

ATHLETIC TICKET OFFICE - (859) 622-2122. Eastern Bypass. Over ten varieties of sports including Collegiate basketball and football.

GREENHOUSE - (859) 622-2228, Eastern Bypass. Foliage propagation and production, rose and carnation beds.

STORY OF A STAR Hummel Planetarium. Special light show for the holidays. (thanksgiving weekend thru December)

FORT BOONESBOROUGH STATE PARK

4375 Boonesborough Road (I-75 exit 95, I-64 exit at Winchester)

Richmond 40475

- ❑ Phone: (859) 527-3131
  http://parks.ky.gov/parks/recreationparks/fort-boonesborough/default.aspx
- ❑ Hours: Wednesday-Sunday 9:00am-5:00pm (April-October). Friday-Sunday 10:00am-4:00pm (rest of year). Closed Thanksgiving and Christmastime.
- ❑ Admission: $5.00-$8.00 (age 6+). November-March admission is minimal as the property is not staffed with re-enactors. Admission includes entrance to both the fort and museum. Additional fee for some activities.
- ❑ Note: Campground, Marina/Boat Launch, Pool, some Hiking Trails, Mini-Golf, Picnicking, and Sandy beach.

After several skirmishes with Indians and rough terrain, Daniel Boone and his men reached the Kentucky River on April 1, 1775 and began laying out Kentucky's 2nd settlement. For many years this was a fortress, stopping point and trade center. The fort they constructed has been reconstructed as a working fort...

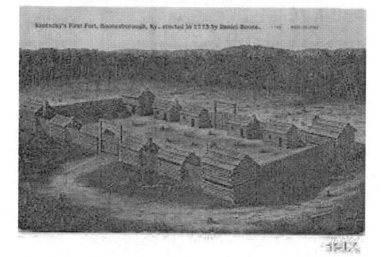

complete with cabins, blockhouses and period furnishings. Resident artisans share pioneer experiences and demonstrate pioneer crafts like pottery, candle-making, weaving and cooking. Riverside trails pass native plants and unusual geological sites. Begin your visit watching a film showing the struggles of the fort - esp. withstanding a 9-day attack by Indians and Frenchmen later known as "The Great Siege". Why are the names Blackfish and Henderson also important here? Look for interesting artifacts like the Clock Rotisserie, giant corn mill, walking spinning wheel or "Pop goes the Weasel".

After leaving Ft. Boonesborough (because of cramped space), Daniel and family moved to a new site just north (I-75 exit 104, off KY 418 east). They suffered many hardships here and several family members are buried at this site. The Kentucky River Museum has numerous displays of prehistoric fishing to locks (some working models) and dams. Steamboats and showboats passed along this River…its visitors and river rats are all explored in this new museum.

RICHMOND CIVIL WAR DRIVING TOUR

345 Lancaster Avenue (Richmond Visitor Center)

Richmond 40475

- ❑   Phone: (859) 626-8474 or (800) 866-3705
  www.trailsrus.com/civilwar/region4/richmond.html
- ❑   Admission: Small fee charged for brochure and tape available
  (for purchase) at the visitor's center.

Follow Confederate troops on a 2 hour driving tour of the battle route of August 1862. There are six tour stations established in the approximate order the battle took place. Begin at the Top of Big Hill and on to places like Mt. Zion Church (used as a Union Hospital) to the Madison County Courthouse. After the Confederate advance, they later marched in triumph into Lexington and then took Frankfort. This was the only time in the war that the capitol of a Union state fell to Southern forces.

WHITE HALL STATE HISTORIC SITE

500 White Hall Shrine Road (I-75 exit 95)

Richmond 40475

- ❑   Phone: (859) 623-9178
  http://parks.ky.gov/parks/historicsites/white-hall/default.aspx
- ❑   Hours: Monday-Saturday 9:00am-5:00pm, Sunday Noon-4pm
  (April-October). No mansion tours on Mondays and Tuesdays.
- ❑   Admission: $8.00 adult, $7.00 senior and $4.00 for students of
  any age.
- ❑   Tours: Last tour begins one hour before closing. One hour long.
- ❑   Note: Gift shop, picnicking.

The home of Cassius Marcellus Clay: emancipationist, newspaper publisher, Minister to Russia, and friend to Abraham Lincoln. Overall, he was quite a character and lived grandly (notice the larger than life doors). Clay's daughter, Laura Clay, was politically active for women's suffrage and states' rights. The restored 44 room Italianate mansion is about 200 years old and has period and heirloom furnishings, a working cookhouse, outside slave/servant quarters, and many unique features for its day. They had running water and central heating (look for the outlets hidden in fireplaces and behind little doors). How were orators (like Clay) similar to our superstars today?

DID YOU KNOW? In 1920, Laura Clay (Cassius' daughter) became the first woman to be nominated for U.S. President by a major political party.

CARR CREEK STATE PARK

PO Box 249 (KY 15 south)

Sassafras 41759

❑   Phone: (606) 642-4050
    http://parks.ky.gov/parks/recreationparks/carr-creek/default.aspx

Camping and the beach are surrounded by mountains and sun. There's also a full-service marina, boating, fishing and rental boats too.

KENTUCKY REPTILE ZOO

200 L & E Railroad (1 mile south of Mountain Pkwy, exit 33 off SR KY 11)

Slade 40376

❑   Phone: (606) 663-9160
    www.kyreptilezoo.org
❑   Hours: Daily 11:00am-6:00pm (Memorial Day-Labor Day).
    Friday-Sunday only 11:00am-6:00pm (March-May, September-October). Weekends in November.
❑   Admission: $10.00 adult, $7.00 child (4-15).

The zoo is also a captive born venom lab with extractions and live reptile presentations held daily on the hour from 1:00-5:00pm. The live reptile exhibits include more than 75 species of lizards, turtles, alligators and snakes. The zoo is now breeding successfully to hopefully use the extracted substances to produce medical and research projects. Look for the vide variety of cobras, rattlesnakes and vipers too.

NATURAL BRIDGE STATE RESORT PARK

2135 Natural Bridge Road (I-64 exit on to the Mountain Parkway
southeast to KY 11)

Slade 40376

- ❏   Phone: (606) 663-2214 or (800) 325-1710 reservations
  **http://parks.ky.gov/parks/resortparks/natural-
  bridge/default.aspx**
- ❏   Hours: Dawn to Dusk
- ❏   Admission: FREE
- ❏   Note: Lodge with dining, Cottages, Campground, Gift Shop,
  Pool, Mini-golf, Picnicking, Weekly Square Dances at Hoe
  Down Islands, Nature Preserve, Mill Creek Lake, Balanced Rock,
  Devil's Gulch, salt peter mines, a cave. Trails End Horse Camp -
  guided horse tours, primitive camping adventures (SR 3330,
  (606) 464-9530). Red River Gorge Geological Area is
  spectacular in its own right!

All we can really say is WOW! Even though we researched this
place for hours before coming to visit - it truly was amazing to
hike or chair lift up to the bridge. A natural sandstone arch, the

bridge spans 78 feet long and 65 feet high. There are no guardrails
(keep a strong hold of children up there…please) and we were one-
third of the way across the Bridge before we realized we were
walking on top of it! The hikes to scenic overlooks and narrow

paths (Fat Man's Misery) were shorter than most, making it very accessible for families. One trail walks you right under the bridge too! May we suggest you try a one-way or round-trip ride on the Natural Bridge Skylift. The Skylift takes you slowly and gradually through some of the most beautiful scenery in the Appalachian area. Sloped gently at first, then a sharp, steep climb up the final stretch - it will leave you mighty anxious to conquer a short trail (600 feet) to the bridge. One way trips are $3.00 (ages 4+) and round-trips are $5.00 for adults and $4.00 for children (4-12). Open Easter weekend thru the end of October at 10:00 am daily. Closing times are posted daily. The whole experience is like a giant amusement park adventure ride!

APPALSHOP

91 Madison Avenue (Hwy 15 bypass to downtown, just past the curve and bridge)

Whitesburg 41858

❑   Phone: (606) 633-0108. **www.appalshop.org**
❑   Admission: FREE
❑   Tours: Guided tours are available by reservation, Monday-Friday 9:00am-5:00pm, closed holidays.

This center focuses on Appalachian culture. They produce a variety of films, videotapes and musical recordings. The highlight for children, on tour, is the stop in the non-commercial community radio station. In the on-hour room the kids can talk on the radio! There is also a visual art exhibit in the gallery for viewing and, depending on the schedule, there may be something going on in the theater or a festival in progress. Stop by on your way out to buy some old-fashioned candy or just listen in on the locals at the Caudill General Store & History Center.

KENTUCKY SPLASH WATER PARK

1050 Hwy 92 West (I-75 exit 11)

Williamsburg 40769

- ❑ Phone: (606) 549-6065. **www.kentuckysplash.com**
- ❑ Hours: Daily, except Sundays 11:00am-7:00pm (Memorial Day weekend thru mid-August). Sundays 12:30-6:30pm. Extended hours for indoor activities.
- ❑ Admission: Waterpark: $10.00 (age 3+). All event: $26.95. Dry activities: $2.00-$5.00 each.

The Hal Rogers Family Entertainment Center is home to the Kentucky Splash Water Park. The park includes an 18,000 square ft. wave pool, a drift river, a kiddy activity pool, a triple slide complex, a go-kart track, a championship miniature golf course, an arcade, a batting cage and even a café and gift shop. Changing rooms/lockers are available.

Chapter 5
Area - West (W)

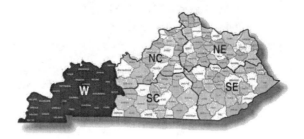

Our Favorites...

* Pratt Memorial Museum - Ft. Campbell

* Land Between the Lakes - Golden Pond

* Trail of Tears - Hopkinsville Area

* State Park Resorts on Lake Barkley & Kentucky Lake

* International Bluegrass Museum - Owensboro

* River Heritage Museum - Paducah

"State Park Trailriding Fun"

A QUICK LOOK AT WESTERN KENTUCKY

There are many casual, comfortable sites and festivals to visit from Fort Campbell to Paducah. The area is full of State Parks, most with camping and lodging. Lake Barkley and the Barkley Dam is where to watch huge barges going through a large lock near Grand Rivers. Slip back in time with a stop in the visitors center for audiovisual exhibits relating to the steamboat era. Then "skipper" your own boat (you can even rent one) or swim in their indoor/outdoor pools. Make it an adventure looking for the tiny Pennyroyal plant out in woodlands at Pennyrile Forest State Resort Park.

If you're still looking for more recreation opportunities, Land Between the Lakes National Recreation Area is located between two major lakes: Kentucky and Barkley. Besides the fun water sports, you'll want to be sure to save time to explore their nature center. Golden Pond Visitors Center, located right in the middle of the area even has a planetarium. Your family can also explore the Elk & Bison Prairie preserve that's 200 years old – mostly grassland and American Indian era animals like bison, elk, deer, wild turkeys, coyotes, rabbits, hawks, owls and songbirds call it home. A drive-thru park has interpretive displays at various spots. Take your kids back to the 1850's at a living history farm (The Homeplace) which recreates the farming and daily activities of a typical rural family living between the Cumberland and Tennessee rivers.

With patriotism running high since September 11th, your family may want to visit the home of the "Screaming Eagles" Airborne Division at Fort Campbell. Probably the best thing to check out is the WWII cargo gliders *(yes, "gliders", what courage!)* displayed in this large military history museum.

Experience the painful fight of Native Americans being forced West from their land at the Heritage Center (and area museums) in Hopkinsville (located along the path of the Trail of Tears). See the gravesites of Chiefs White Path and Fly Smith. In September, the town has a traditional Indian Pow-Wow where you can watch tribal dancing, listen to storytelling and eat Native American food.

Paducah may be famous for quilts, but they have much river heritage too. Overlooking the confluence of the Tennessee and Ohio Rivers stands the Center for Maritime Education. View river navigation simulations in progress from the observation deck. See interactive (permanent and changing) exhibits that tell the story of the Four Rivers Region, a geographic area that encompasses the Ohio, Cumberland, Tennessee and Mississippi Rivers.

A famous native of the area is Jefferson Davis. His Birthday Celebration in Fairview is a living history celebration honoring the Confederate President on his birthday (in June) at his birthplace. The 351 foot obelisk is the fourth tallest in the world with an elevator to the top for viewing.

Dotted throughout Southwest Kentucky are numerous "home town" railroad museums. If you like railroading artifacts, locals can tell you a story to match every piece on display.

Western Chapter at a Glance...

Calvert City
- KY Lake Motor Speedway

Columbus
- Columbus-Belmont St Pk

Dawson Springs
- Pennyrile Forest St Resort Pk

Dunmor
- Dogwood Lakes
- Lake Malone St Pk

Fairview
- Jefferson Davis Monument

Fort Campbell
- Pratt Memorial / Wings of Liberty

Grand Rivers

- Patti's 1880s Settlement

Guthrie
- Robert Penn Warren BP

Hardin
- Kenlake St Pk

Henderson
- John James Audubon St Pk
- WC Handy Blues & BBQ Fest

Hopkinsville
- Trail of Tears Pk

Land Between the Lakes
- KY Opry
- Lake Barkley St Pk
- Venture River Waterpk
- Mineral Mound St Pk

- KY Dam Village
- Maggie's Jungle Golf
- Land Betw the Lakes Natl Rec Area

Marion

- Clement Mineral Museum

Murray

- Playhouse in the Park

Owensboro

- Owensboro Mus of Science & History
- Internatl Bluegrass Music Museum
- Internatl BBQ Fest
- Apple Festival-Reids Orchard
- Holiday in the Park

Paducah

- Market House Theatre
- Natl Quilt Museum
- Paducah Internatl Raceway
- River Heritage Museum
- Floodwall Murals
- Whitehaven Welcome Ctr
- William Clark Market House
- Yeiser Art Ctr

Princeton

- Adsmore House Museum

Wickliffe

- Wickliffe Mounds

KENTUCKY LAKE MOTOR SPEEDWAY

950 Truck Plaza (I-24 exit 27 to the Interstate Frontage Road)

Calvert City 42029

❑   Phone: (270) 395-3600. **www.kylakespeedway.com**

Dirt track racing, monster trucks, truck/tractor pulls, rodeos and occasional concerts. Many NASCAR races including late models, open wheel modified and limited sportsmen plus sprint. Saturday nights (March-October)

COLUMBUS-BELMONT STATE PARK

350 Park Road (36 miles southwest of Paducah on KY 80 & KY 58)

Columbus 42032

❑   Phone: (270) 677-2327
     http://parks.ky.gov/parks/recreationparks/columbus-belmont/default.aspx

- ❑ Hours: 9:00am-5:00pm daily (May-September). Weekends only (April & October).
- ❑ Admission: Park is FREE. Museum is $2-$4 per person.
- ❑ Note: Campground, Gift shop, Boat launches and marina, hiking trails, mini-golf, picnicking.

Columbus-Belmont State Park is a National Scenic Byway and National Trail of Tears Site. It is also on the Civil War Heritage Trail.

Recall the 1861 Battle of Belmont and the fight to control this important waterway called the "Gibraltar of the West". But a General named Grant outflanked the "Gibraltar" and forced its evacuation. See the massive chain and anchor used by the South to block passage of the Union gunboats and the earthen trenches dug to protect almost 20,000 Confederate troops. The museum was once a Civil War hospital but now serves as a display of Indian artifacts and Civil War relics. A video is shown.

CIVIL WAR DAYS Columbus-Belmont SP. The living history presentations portray Grant's first assignment at a strategic location for control of the Mississippi River. They formed a Confederate "chain of men" and this is re-enacted. Authentic sutlers, music, food. Night firing of the cannons and Sunday church services. (second weekend in October)

PENNYRILE FOREST STATE RESORT PARK

20781 Pennyrile Lodge Road
(KY 109N, 20 miles NW of Hopkinsville)

Dawson Springs 42408

- ❑ Phone: (270) 797-3421 lodge or (800) 325-1711 reservations
  http://parks.ky.gov/parks/resortparks/pennyrile-forest/default.aspx

Named for the Pennyroyal plant found in the surrounding woodlands, the place is good for a rustic get-a-way by lodge or cottage. The rustic wood and stone lodge, with 24 rooms, sits serenely on a high cliff overlooking Pennyrile Lake. The park has 13 cottages located in the wooded lodge area and on the shores of

Pennyrile Lake. The one and two-bedroom cottages have unique features, offering wooded or lake views, and such amenities as private boat and fishing docks, fireplaces, or screened-in porches. Also available are mountain biking trails, campground, gift shop, boat rentals, hiking trials, tennis, mini-golf, and programs.

DOGWOOD LAKES RESORT & FUNPARK

777 State Route 973 (2 miles from Lake Malone, US 431S)

Dunmor 42339

❑ Phone: (270) 657-8380.
  http://facebook.com/dogwoodcampingresort/
❑ Hours: Basically 11:00am-5:00pm (Memorial Day weekend thru first full week of August). open most long weekends (Special events, May- mid-September).
❑ Admission: Gate & Swimming: $4.00-$5.00 (age 3+). Slides additional fee ($6.50 - $12.00 armbands) . wkends only.
❑ Note: Many special events like Country Jam (June), Gospel Day (August). Concession stand and gift shop. Activities for kids on weekends.

Relax and enjoy the beach on one of three clear lakes. Play and splash on the swimming decks, paddle boats, kiddie play area or waterslides. Full hook-up camp sites and Top Dog Camping Sheds are available for overnights.

LAKE MALONE STATE PARK

PO Box 93 (from Greenville, take US 431 south to KY 973)

Dunmor 42339

❑ Phone: (270) 657-2111
  http://parks.ky.gov/parks/recreationparks/lake-malone/default.aspx

This small park is enclosed by a 200-foot sandstone bluff and hardwood forest. The park has a campground, marina, beach, rental boats and hiking trails. The mile and one-half Laurel Trail is an easy-rated hiking trail providing views of many rock walls, once used as shelters by prehistoric Native Americans.

JEFFERSON DAVIS MONUMENT STATE HISTORIC SITE

258 Pembroke-Fairview Rd (US 68 east), **Fairview** 42221

❏   Phone: (270) 889-6100

     http://parks.ky.gov/parks/historicsites/jefferson-davis/

❏   Hours: Daily 9:00am-5:00pm (April thru mid-November).

❏   Admission to Museum or Monument: $4.00 for Adults; $3.00 for 55+, military, and ages 5 - 12; 4 & under FREE. Combination Museum and Monument: $8 Adults; $6 Military & Seniors & child (Ages 5-12).

The name Jefferson Davis is best known as the man elected President of the Confederate States of America in 1861 preceding the Civil War. Ironically, both Davis and Abraham Lincoln were born in Kentucky in log cabins within one year and 100 miles apart. A 351 obelisk marks the birthplace of Jefferson Davis, born here on June 3, 1808. The monument features an elevator to the top of the structure for a panoramic view of the surrounding countryside. The visitor center enlightens visitors on the unique history that caused its preservation. A short DVD presentation and exhibits detail the political life of Davis before and after the Civil War and the building of the monument. Also told is the little known story of the Kentucky "Orphan Brigade." The center includes a gift shop featuring Kentucky handcrafts, souvenirs, books and Civil War memorabilia.

JEFFERSON DAVIS BIRTHDAY CELEBRATION Jefferson Davis State Historic Site. A living history celebration honors the Confederate President on his birthday at his birthplace. The 351 foot obelisk is the 4th tallest in the world with an elevator to the top for viewing. (first weekend in June)

PRATT MEMORIAL MUSEUM/WINGS OF LIBERTY

Bldg. 5702, Tennessee Ave. (Ft. Campbell, US 41A, Gate 4 entrance), **Fort Campbell 42241**

- ❏ Phone: (270) 798-3215 or (270) 798-4986
  www.fortcampbell.com/wolmm.php
- ❏ Hours: Daily 9:30am-4:30pm. Be sure to check hours before you visit. The museum is in transition from old to new. Closed Christmas and New Years. Central Time
- ❏ Admission: FREE

Probably the best thing to check out are the WW II cargo gliders displayed on this large military reservation museum. Exhibits on the history of Ft. Campbell and the many units stationed here from the present back to World War II include: uniforms, photos, restored aircraft and some weapons. There's even a display with Adolph Hitler's walking stick. The new, **WINGS OF LIBERTY MILITARY MUSEUM** will open to positively replace the current structure. It will be located directly off US 41A. The approximately 80,000 square feet facility includes a 200-seat IMAX-style theater, art gallery, cafe, book store/gift shop, and an artifact storage area. The main exhibit area will display artifacts ranging from the WWII D-Day invasion of Normandy to Operation Desert Shield/Desert Storm in Kuwait and Iraq and operations in Panama, Somalia, Haiti, and Bosnia.

DID YOU KNOW? Ft. Campbell is home to the 101st Airborne Division (known as the "Screaming Eagles"), the 5th Special Forces Group and the 160th Special Operations Aviation Regiment.

KENTUCKY OPRY

US Hwy 641N

Land Between the Lakes (Benton) 42025

- ❏ Phone: (270)- 527-3869 **www.kentuckyopry.com**
- ❏ Hours: Shows Every Friday night during the months of June, July, August & December. Shows Every Saturday Night Year Round. Central Time. Shows begin at 7:30pm.

❑   Admission: ~$11.00 adults, ~Half-price children

This show presents some of the finest talent in Kentucky. It's wholesome entertainment for the entire family - featuring country, gospel, down-home comedy and Bluegrass music.

LAKE BARKLEY STATE RESORT PARK

Box 790 (US 68W to KY 1489)

Land Between the Lakes (Cadiz) 42211

❑   Phone: (800) 325-1708, (270) 924-1131 Lodge, (800) 295-1878
      Marina. **http://parks.ky.gov/parks/resortparks/lake-barkley/default.aspx**
❑   Note: Eagles Weekend late February. Offering eagle viewing
      trips and live animal evening programs. Admission.

The world-class lodge of post-and-beam wood construction with lots of windows for viewing is what most think of when mentioning Barkley. A spacious campground, lighted airstrip and Fitness Center with indoor/outdoor pools are favorites too. The Barkley Dam is where to watch barges going through a large lock off KY 453 near Grand Rivers and stop in the center for audiovisual exhibits relating to the steamboat era. For private accommodations, enjoy one of the nine two-bedroom, two-bath cottages with lake or wooded views. For rustic charm, Lake Barkley offers 4 two-bedroom log cabins. Each have unique appeal, and offer screened-in porches or decks. Tableware, cooking utensils and fresh linens are provided. Also on the premises are a marina, camping, boat rentals, horseback riding, tennis and recreation programs.

HAM FESTIVAL

Cadiz. Highlight is cooking of the world's largest ham and biscuit sandwich (Guinness Record). Top name performers and food. **Www.hamfestival.com** (second weekend in October)

VENTURE RIVER WATER PARK

280 Park Place (I-24 exit 40, US 62)

Land Between the Lakes (Eddyville) 42038

❏ Phone: (270) 388-7999. **www.ventureriver.com**

❏ Hours: Daily 10:00am-7:00pm (Summer). Central Time

❏ Admission: $18-$25 average general admission (age 3+). Seniors
     & After 4:00pm are about half of the price.

With kiddie rides added to five body slides, two tube slides, a
Wave Pool, cyclone, kiddie pool, Frog Island, action river, and
beach volleyball - there's plenty of summertime fun. Waloopas
twin enclosed water slides are the newest feature.

MINERAL MOUND STATE PARK

(off US62/641, KY 93 south of Eddyville, north of the I-24 exit)

Land Between the Lakes (Eddyville) 42044

❏ Phone: (270) 362-4271 Kentucky Dam
     **http://parks.ky.gov/parks/recreationparks/mineral-
     mound/default.aspx**

On the shores of Lake Barkley, this park is historically linked to
the author F. Scott Fitzgerald - this was once the farm of
Fitzgerald's wife's grandfather. Boat launch, some hiking trails.

KENTUCKY DAM VILLAGE STATE RESORT PARK

PO Box 69 (I-24 east to exit 27, US 62 to US 641east)

Land Between the Lakes (Gilbertsville) 42044

❏ Phone: (270) 362-4271 Lodge, (800) 325-0146 reservations,
     (270) 362-8386 Marina.
     **http://parks.ky.gov/parks/resortparks/ky-dam-
     village/default.aspx**

❏ Note: Gathering of Eagles Weekend in mid-January. Viewing
     and learning eagle spotting techniques and finding their habitats.

This is one of three resort parks surrounding Land Between the Lakes National Recreation Area. With an abundance of water, the most popular sports are boating, water-skiing, snorkeling and fishing. The main lodge has private balconies or patios and fine dining. With 68 cottages, Kentucky Dam Village has more choices for overnight accommodations than any other state park. You can choose a one, two, or three-bedroom cottage with one or two baths. Tableware, cooking utensils, and fresh linens are provided. There's also a campground, gift shop, airport, marina, boat rentals, pool, beach, tennis, mini-golf and recreation programs.

EARTH DAY CELEBRATION - NATIVE AMERICAN HERITAGE DAY/ANNUAL BUFFALO DINNER Kentucky Dam Village - Enjoy a weekend filled with opportunities to learn about the Native American culture through demonstrations of storytelling, hands-on pottery, bow making, basket weaving and displays from Wickliffe Mounds. Fee for dinner. (Earth Day, late April)

MAGGIE'S JUNGLE GOLF & JUNGLE RUN

7301 US Hwy 641 N (near Kentucky Dam), **Land Between the Lakes (Gilbertsville) 42044**

- ❑ Phone: (270) 362-8933   **http://maggiesjunglegolf.com**
- ❑ Hours: Call for seasonal hours and admission pricing.
- ❑ Admission: Generally $4.00 per person. Cost per Jungle Run is $2 per person to walk or you may rent a cart for $8 that seats max. of 2 adults and 3 small children. Drivers must be 16 years of age with a valid Drivers license.

Putt-putt at its best. Enjoy a combination of shuffleboard, putt-putt and live animals with a petting zoo, nature trail, covered bridges and a picnic area or take a ride in the Safari Car. The nature trail has pygmy goats, llamas, pot-bellied pigs, camel, and miniature horses.

LAND BETWEEN THE LAKES NATIONAL RECREATION AREA

100 Van Morgan Drive (I-24w exit 31, SRKY 453 south to the Trace on US 68/KY80 between Kentucky Lake and Lake Barkley)

Land Between the Lakes (Golden Pond) 42211

- ❑ Phone: (270) 924-2020. **www.lbl.org**
- ❑ Hours: Open year-round but some facilities are closed during winter. See specific facility hours below. Central Time.
- ❑ Admission: FREE, except specific facilities listed below.
- ❑ Note: Kentucky Kayak Kountry Phone: 270-362-0081.

"Land Between the Lakes" located between:

- ❑ **KENTUCKY LAKE** - a top fishing , water sport and water recreation area on the largest lake in Kentucky. Over 2300 miles of shoreline with the Kentucky Dam (US 62/641) at Gilbertsville across the Tenn. River is 208 ft. high and 8400 ft. wide.
- ❑ **LAKE BARKLEY** – 2nd largest Kentucky lake with 1000 miles of shoreline for recreation and the lake for fishing. The Barclay Dam is off KY 453 near Grand Rivers across the Cumberland River.

Facilities available:

- ❑ **GOLDEN POND VISITORS CENTER** - centrally located, has info, displays, a planetarium and video orientation. Open 9:00am-5:00pm, year-round, except Thanksgiving, Christmas and New Year's. Planetarium admission is between $2.00-$4.00.

- ❑ **ELK & BISON PRAIRIE** - 1 mile north on the Trace. 750 acre preserve is a recreation of the prairie that existed over 200 years ago - mostly grassland and American Indian era animals like bison, elk, deer, wild turkeys, coyotes, rabbits, hawks, owls and songbirds. A drive-thru park with interpretive displays at various spots. Daily dawn-dusk. Admission $5.00 per vehicle.

- ❑ **THE HOMEPLACE** - 15 miles south on the Trace (actually in Tennessee, just over the border). A living-history farm which re-creates the farming and daily activities of a typical rural family living between the Cumberland and Tennessee rivers in the 1850s.

❑   Interpreters are dressed in period clothing and talk to guests
      while doing daily chores. There are 16 buildings (some original),
      an interpretive center with exhibits and video orientation, and
      many seasonal festivals most every weekend. Monday-Saturday
      9:00am-5:00pm, Sunday 10:00am-5:00pm (April-October);
      Closed Mondays and Tuesdays in March and November.
      Admission $4 adults, $2.00 children (5-12).

❑   **THE NATURE STATION** - north on the Trace, then east on
      Mulberry Flat Road, follow signs. An environmental education
      center offering canoe rentals, trails and live animal exhibits.
      Special weekend events March thru November. Bald eagle
      viewing excursions by boat and van in the winter months. Open
      Monday-Saturday 9am-5pm, Sunday 10am-5pm (April-October);
      Closed Mondays and Tuesdays in March and November. Area is
      FREE but Nature Station is $4 adults, $2.00 children (5-12).

PATTI'S 1880'S SETTLEMENT

1793 J.H. O'Bryan Drive (I-24 exit 31 south)

Grand Rivers 42045

❑   Phone: (270) 362-8844 or (888) 736-2515
      www.pattis-settlement.com
❑   Hours: Open daily 10:30am-8:00pm. Central time. Moderate
      prices. Children's menu.

Relaxed dining in 1880s atmosphere featuring homemade pies,
flower pot bread and 2" thick pork chops. Historic log cabin
settlement with unique shops, miniature golf, rock climbing wall,
remote control boats & cars, summer concerts, and animal park.
Try the mile-high lemon meringue pie, Bill's Boatsinker or
Sawdust pie.

ROBERT PENN WARREN BIRTHPLACE MUSEUM

Corner of Third and Cherry Streets

Guthrie 42234

❑   Phone: (270) 483-2683
      www.robertpennwarren.com/birthpla.html

- ❏ Hours: Tuesday-Saturday 11:30am-3:30pm, Sunday 2:00-4:00pm. Closed holidays. Central time.
- ❏ Admission: Donations

Here is the boyhood home of America's first poet laureate, Robert Penn Warren, author of 10 novels and 16 volumes of poetry. Warren lived here in the early 1900's until age 16. Warren is best known for his fiction novel " All the King's Men" (Pulitzer 1946). Inspire your children by viewing photos, books and works of the author on display.

KENLAKE STATE RESORT PARK

542 Kenlake Road (I-24 north, exit US 68/KY 80W OR I-24 to Purchase Pkwy, then US 68E)

Hardin 42048

- ❏ Phone: (800) 325-0143 reservations, Lodge (270) 474-2211. Marina (270) 474-2245
  http://parks.ky.gov/parks/resortparks/kenlake/default.aspx
- ❏ Note: Eagle weekend early February. View bald eagle in natural habitat. Evening programs and refreshments. Admission.

Located on the western shore of Kentucky Lake, this park features an indoor tennis center and pro shop, 200 miles of woodland trails and a grand hotel. For more private accommodations, you may choose a one, two, or three-bedroom cottage with one or two baths. These cottages offer beautiful lake, wooded, or golf course views with features that include decks and screened-in porches. Tableware, cooking utensils, and linens are provided. Also campgrounds, marina, boat rentals, a pool, horseback riding trails and recreation programs.

JOHN JAMES AUDUBON STATE PARK

3100 US Hwy 41N (US 41 north, near Ohio River)

Henderson 42420

- ❏ Phone: (270) 826-2247 or (270) 827-1893 Center
  http://parks.ky.gov/parks/recreationparks/john-james/default.aspx

- ❑ Hours: Park open dawn to dusk. Center open 10:00am-5:00pm daily except Winter holidays. Central Time.
- ❑ Admission: a small admission may be charged.

Named for the first naturalist to artistically portray and protect birds - this is where he observed the subjects of his paintings from 1810-1819. Part of the Mississippi Flyway of migration, the Museum & Center seek to interpret Audubon's life through his original art, personal memorabilia, bird observation areas and the Discovery area with hands-on exhibits and educational themed programs. A giant bird's nest is the centerpiece of the hands-on area. Be sure to look for a lovely souvenir reprint of his works - most notably the great horned owl and woodpecker series. Also found on site are campgrounds, small rental cottages, rental boats, hiking trails, golf and mini-golf, tennis and lots of birding and fishing.

W C HANDY BLUES AND BARBEQUE FESTIVAL

Henderson. **www.handyblues.org** The legendary blues musician and composer is honored by his hometown community with jazz music and mouthwatering barbecue. Music at the festival includes a wide variety of blues styles, from gritty delta blues to smooth soul to big horn bands. This festival has become one of the largest FREE music festivals in the nation, drawing folks from almost every state and many countries. (Entire second full week in June)

TRAIL OF TEARS COMMEMORATIVE PARK

US 41 South, Pembroke Road

Hopkinsville 42240

- ❑ Phone: (270) 886-8033. **www.trailoftears.org**
- ❑ Hours: Park open during daylight hours, daily. Heritage Center: Thursday-Saturday 10:00am-2:00pm.

This historic park is one of the few documented sites of actual trail and campsites used during the forced removal of the Cherokee people to "Indian Territory". It was used as an encampment in 1838 and 1839. The Park is situated on a portion of the campground used by the Cherokees on the infamous Trail of Tears and includes the gravesites of Chiefs White Path and Fly Smith. The park includes a Heritage Center, picnic areas and ample parking.

TRAIL OF TEARS INDIAN POW-WOW. Trail of Tears Park. A sad period in our country's history is remembered with tribal dancing, Native American storytelling and food. Meet Chiefs Whitepath and Fly Smith and stop in the Heritage Museum to view cultural displays. Www.trailoftears.org. Admission. (weekend after Labor Day)

CLEMENT MINERAL MUSEUM

205 North Walker Street

Marion 42064

❑   Phone: (270) 965-4263
     www.clementmineralmuseum.org
❑   Hours: Wednesday-Saturday 10:00am-3:00pm. Closed all
     holidays and last week of December. Central time
❑   Admission: $3.00-$5.00

This is the area where 19th century pirates once robbed flatboats along the river.   In the museum are more than 30,000 native mineral specimens shown in 5 different exhibit areas. The fluorite crystals with a blacklight show is a must see. They have digs in surrounding area every month. Feelin lucky?

PLAYHOUSE IN THE PARK

Gil Hopson Drive (corner of Arcadia & 8th street, Central Park)
Murray 42071

❑   Phone: (270) 759-1752   **www.playhouseinthepark.net**
❑   Hours: Year-round productions are performed Thursday-Saturday
     evenings and Sunday matinees. Central time.

Family entertainment of comedies, musicals (like Heidi), dramas and mysteries. Box of Frogs Childrens Theatre.

WESTERN KENTUCKY HIGHLAND FESTIVAL
Murray City Park, Central Park. Celebration of Scottish-Celtic heritage featuring all things Scottish such as: bagpipe bands, music, amateur athletic competition including: caber-tossing, sheath toss, weighted throws, stone throws, etc., Clan tents, Scottish entertainers, genealogy tent, Scottish vendors, highland cattle, sheepherding. **Www.murraykyhighlandgames.com** (first Saturday in October)

OWENSBORO MUSEUM OF SCIENCE AND HISTORY

220 Daviess Street (off US 60)

Owensboro 42302

❑   Phone: (270) 687-2732 **www.owensboromuseum.com**
❑   Hours: Tuesday-Saturday 10:00am-5:00pm, Sunday 1:00-
     5:00pm. Central time.
❑   Admission: $3.00 general, $10.00 family.

The science aspect focuses on disciplines like astronomy, geology and botany. Cultural aspects of archeology, county history and Native Americans are explored too. Of special interest to children is the live reptile collection, the Government Education Center featuring exhibits that explain how government works, and a children's hands-on exhibit. The areas are divided into Speedzeum, Coal Mine, PlayZeum, and Encounter.

INTERNATIONAL BLUEGRASS MUSIC MUSEUM

117 Daviess Street (RiverPark Center)

Owensboro 42303

❑   Phone: (270) 926-7891. **www.bluegrass-museum.org**
❑   Hours: Tuesday-SAturday 10:00am-5:00pm, Sunday 1:00-
     4:00pm. Closed January and February.
❑   Admission: $5.00 adult, $2.00 student (age 7-16).

Visit the Bluegrass Hall of Honor, a heritage theatre and new interactive exhibits. View a showcase of historically significant bluegrass instruments, meet the varieties of cultures evolving the roots of bluegrass, or listen to a bluegrass jukebox. Create your own bluegrass mix in the studio or stand under "listening domes" situated throughout the concourse.

INTERNATIONAL BAR-B-Q FESTIVAL

Owensboro. Downtown. Cooking teams compete to make the finest barbecued mutton, chicken and thousands of gallons of burgoo as judged and consumed by the public. Smoke from hickory-stoked fires blends with the aromas of sizzling chicken, bubbling burgoo and roasting mutton to complete the festival atmosphere. Also games, contests and country dancing. **www.bbqfest.com** (second weekend in May)

APPLE FESTIVAL

Owensboro. Reids Orchard (KY 144). **www.reidorchard.com** An abundance of apples are featured in a carnival, crafts, petting zoo, hayrides, pick-u-own and apple food and cider. (third weekend in October)

HOLIDAY IN THE PARK

Owensboro. Legion Park. Stroll through the park and you will surely become filled with the holiday spirit. Giant elves, trees, toys and figures, not to mention Santa in his sleigh, line Legion's half-mile walking path. This year the park will come alive as your favorite structures dace to holiday music. (270) 687-8700. (December)

MARKET HOUSE THEATRE

132 Market House Square

Paducah 42001

❑   Phone: (270) 444-6828 or (888) MHT-PLAY
      www.mhtplay.com

15-20 productions per season of comedy, musicals and children's shows like The Velveteen Rabbit or Annie Jr. and the Children's Choir.

NATIONAL QUILT MUSEUM

215 Jefferson Street (I-24 Downtown Loop)

Paducah 42001

❑   Phone: (270) 442-8856. **www.quiltmuseum.org**
❑   Hours: Monday-Saturday 10:00am-5:00pm year round. Sunday
     1:00-5:00pm (March-November). Closed all Winter and Spring
     holidays. Central Time.
❑   Admission: $11.00 adult, $10.00 senior (60+), $5.00 student (age
     12+).
❑   Note: Gift shop and bookstore.

Changing theme exhibits display over 200 quilts from old-
fashioned to modern to colorful to unique or abstract. The building
has eight stained glass windows with designs based on quilt
patterns.

PADUCAH INTERNATIONAL RACEWAY

4445 Shemwell Lane

Paducah 42001

❑   Phone: (270) 898-7469. **www.paducahracing.com**
❑   Hours: Some Friday and most every Saturday night beginning at
     7:00pm, gates open at 4:00pm (May-October) Central time.

A 3/8 mile, high bank dirt track. Racing, late model, modified, pre-
stock and street stock autos.

RIVER HERITAGE MUSEUM & FLOODWALL MURALS

117 S. Water Street (RiverPlace)

Paducah 42001

❑   Phone: (270) 575-9958 **www.steamboats.org/traveller/ohio-
     river/paducah.html**
❑   Hours: Monday-Saturday 9:30am-5:00pm, Sunday 1:00-5:00pm.
❑   Admission: $5.00 adult, $3.00 child (3-12).
❑   Tours: By reservation

Overlooking the confluence of the Tennessee and Ohio Rivers stands the Center for Maritime Education. View river navigation simulation in progress from an observation deck. Exhibits tell the story of the Four Rivers Region, a geographic area that encompasses the Ohio, Cumberland, Tennessee and Mississippi Rivers. The museum features water-filled exhibits including a working lock and dam model. A build-a-river exhibit allows the visitor to maneuver sand and water to form various river configurations. A dredging exhibit shows how the sediment of river bottoms is moved in order to improve navigational channels. This exhibit also features various samples of mussel species. Mud microscopes enable the visitor to view the river bottoms.

Across the street, Western Kentucky's rich heritage comes alive on **FLOODWALL MURALS** (800-Paducah) painted by Muralist, Robert Dafford. The floodwalls have vivid scenes painted from history include the Standing Watch View From the Pilot House, the Christening of the Eleanor, and the Visit of the Three "Queens" to Paducah. (The American Queen, the Delta Queen and the Mississippi Queen.) Bronze interpretive panels explain the content and enable onlookers to understand the content of each mural.

WHITEHAVEN WELCOME CENTER

Kentucky Welcome Center (I-24E exit 7, US 45)

Paducah 42001

- ❑ Phone: (270) 554-2077 or (800) 225-TRIP
  http://www.aboutpaducah.com/articles/whitehaven-welcome-center.html
- ❑ Hours: Daily 8:00am-6:00pm. Central time.
- ❑ Admission: FREE
- ❑ Tours: Daily on the half hour 1:00-4:00pm
- ❑ Note: Modern restroom facilities open 24 hours.

Whitehaven mansion was built in the mid-1800s and the historical tourist center is designed to offer a glimpse of the state's past and symbolize Kentucky's position as a gateway to the South. Exhibits highlight Paducah native, Alben Barkley, Senator and US Vice-President.

WILLIAM CLARK MARKET HOUSE MUSEUM

121 South Second Street (Center of the Market House Square)

Paducah 42001

❑   Phone: (270) 443-7759 **http://markethousemueum.com**
❑   Hours: Monday-Saturday Noon-4:00pm. Closed in January & February and major holidays. Central Time.
❑   Admission: $1.00-$4.00 (age 6+).

Articles displayed from Paducah's history in the 1905 Market House. Find inside an 1870's drug store, Civil War relics, river and local history exhibits.

YEISER ART CENTER

200 Broadway Street

Paducah 42001

❑   Phone: (270) 442-2453. **www.theyeiser.org**
❑   Hours: Tuesday-Saturday 10:00am-4:00pm Closed major holidays. Central time. FREE admission.

Changing exhibitions of Kentucky and national artists, contemporary and historical art forms, painting, photography, sculpture, prints, mixed media, fibers. National Fibers Exhibit each spring. Call ahead for the Elements in Art handout that helps your children understand the basics of art in every work they view. The art appreciation card can be utilized with any exhibit that they sponsor. The card can be used by the child alone or with an adult. It provides information based on the elements of art, poses questions, and suggests that the child interact (visually) with the works. They also have interactive panels that are hands on. They show an example of a recognized work of art and then invite the children to draw, paint, touch, or move items to illustrate the various concepts shown on the panels.

ADSMORE HOUSE MUSEUM

304 North Jefferson Street

Princeton 42445

❑   Phone: (270) 365-3114 **www.adsmore.org**
❑   Hours: Tuesday-Saturday 11:00am-4:00pm, Sunday 1:00-
        4:00pm. Central time.
❑   Admission: $7.00 adult, $6.00 senior (65+), $2.00 child (6-12).

A c. 1857 Greek Revival home restored to late Victorian. Period-
costumed guides give the feeling of that place and time. The
Gunshop is restored to 1844 to tell the story of Princeton's first
gunsmith. Scenes portray a funeral, a wedding, the Night Riders
1906 raid, or Christmas 1901.

BATTLE OF SACRAMENTO

Sacramento. This large re-enactment takes place on the original
battlefield where Confederate Gen. Nathan Forrest and his bunch
of 300 men won the day (Dec. 1861). Old-time demonstrations,
dulcimer   musicians,   field   hospitals,   special   guests.
www.battleofsac.com (third weekend in May)

WICKLIFFE MOUNDS

94 Green Street (northwest on US 51 / 60 / 62)

Wickliffe 42087

❑   Phone: (270) 335-3681
        **http://parks.ky.gov/parks/historicsites/wickliffe-
        mounds/default.aspx**
❑   Hours: Daily 9:00am-4:30pm (May-September). Wednesday-
        Sunday only (March, April, October and November). Central
        Time.
❑   Admission: $5.00 adult, $4.00 senior (55+), $4.00 child (6-11).
❑   Educators: Teachers Packet w/ sctivities and scavenger hunt:
        **http://parks.ky.gov/!userfiles/wickliffe-mounds/wickliffe-
        mounds-teachers-packet-2015.pdf**

This Research Center and Archeological Site is where they've
excavated   prehistoric   (1100-1350AD)   Mississippian   Mound
culture villages.

Located on a bluff overlooking the Mississippi river, the village was occupied from about AD 1100 to 1350.

Unearthed for current viewing is a burial mound, home sites and temple mounds with different interpretive exhibits that illustrate prehistoric Indian life and also explain how the archeologists do their work. The Ceremonial Mound is intact and can be accessed for a beautiful bird's eye view of the park. A Hands-On Activity Touch Table rounds out a museum tour where visitors can use prehistoric tools, and learn about Mississippian artifacts, technology and their environment.

AMUSEMENTS

ANIMALS & FARMS

KENTUCKY HISTORY

For updates visit our website: www.kidslovetravel.com

SPORTS

THE ARTS

For updates visit our website: www.kidslovetravel.com

TOURS

LODGING & DINING